Modern Scribes and Lettering Artists

Modern Scribes and Lettering Artists

A Pentalic Book, Taplinger Publishing Company, New York

First Paperback Edition
Published in the United States in 1983 by
Taplinger Publishing Co., Inc.
New York, New York

Copyright © Trefoil Books Ltd.
Printed in Great Britain

Book designer: Langley Iddins
Cover illustration by Martin Jackson

Library of Congress Catalog Card
Number: 80-50362
ISBN 0-8008-5297-4
ISBN 0-8008-5298-2 (pbk.)

Contents

Acknowledgements

The publishers wish to thank in particular Sue Cavendish and The Society of Scribes & Illuminators, London for all their patient work and enthusiasm and the following societies for their co-operation: Calligraphy Space 2001, New York City; Chicago Calligraphy Collective; Colleagues of Calligraphy, St Paul, Minnesota; Friends of Calligraphy, San Francisco; Lettering Arts Guild of Boston; Opulent Order of Practising Scribes, Roswell, New Mexico; Philadelphia Calligraphers Society; Society for Calligraphy, Los Angeles; British Columbian Branch of the Society for Italic Handwriting; Society of Scribes, New York City; The Society for Italic Handwriting, London; Washington Calligraphers Guild; Western American Branch of the Society for Italic Handwriting.

Artwork by Robert Boyajian, Tony Di Spigna, Charles Pearce, Mary Quinault Kossakowski, Marcy Robinson, John Skelton, St Clair Richard, Patricia Weisberg, Wendy Westover is copyright © 1980 of the respective artists.

While every effort has been made to correctly credit sources apologies are made for any omissions.

Introduction

Letters and words are everywhere about us. They direct and inform us, often so unconsciously that we are unaware of their potency and power, recording the loftiest and most banal thoughts of mankind. And in writing we all make our own, a love letter, a signature, a shopping list, sometimes with care and an eye for beauty, sometimes illegibly. Those letters around us, in the street or on the printed page, are all made and designed by someone somewhere. Only occasionally are these made by hand. The dullness and insensitivity of much mechanically produced lettering, and all letters should be gay or sad, exuberant or restrained, or whatever is appropriate to a particular situation, is a sad comment on our times. Yet in so many other ways we live in times that are vigorous and individually vital.

This book is concerned with handmade lettering and calligraphy, some 'one off' pieces of work executed for a particular person or place, some made for reproduction to appear multiplied in many hundreds or thousands in a particular context. That the book has been published is a reflection of the widespread interest in handmade lettering in many parts of the world. More and more people are turning to the sensuous enjoyment of the manipulation of tools and materials in the creation of written and lettered things, physical expressions of intellectual and tactile responses to words and lettershapes.

In this book will be found many and varied examples of lettering in a number of media, parchment, paper, stone, glass, metal and wood, made by a number of craftsmen from many countries, of all levels of experience and expertise. There is work by professional craftsmen and letterers, some of whom have studied and practised their craft for many years, as well as work by enthusiastic amateur craftsmen who, though some may lack the expertise of the professionals, yield nothing in freshness and enthusiasm for their work. This is important because although a professional artist with a skill developed from everyday familiarity with his tools and materials may be capable of producing work with a verve denied the amateur, the amateur unfettered by financial pressures may allow himself to consider work at leisure, its problems and possibilities, and to experiment with techniques and materials in a manner denied the professional.

The reproductions of the work given in this book have been divided into three parts, original lettering and calligraphy, work cut or incised into stone or other material, and lettering made specifically for reproduction. All the work has been carried out since 1976. It must be remembered that each category possesses different qualities and that some of these are bound to be lost in reproduction.

The work made for reproduction, as might be expected, shows best in the book and it is the only work that originally may have been worked upon larger than the size it was designed to appear. It is also the only work that might have been carefully built up, parts added or removed and otherwise altered until judged ready for use. In this way handmade lettering for reproduction can lose something of the qualities of being handmade and present a misleading impression of perfection of finish.

The original calligraphic work loses most in reproduction as the very qualities that are most valued in it cannot be reproduced. The potency of the artist's hand, the actual strokes of pen or brush on skin or paper, will cast a spell over the spectator. The subtlety of the intimate relationship between object and spectator will always differ from person to person according to light and mood, but these can only be enjoyed in front of an original. But then the last is true of any lettered object whether made for public display or private enjoyment.

Much of the work in the book reveals the influence of the broad-edged tool, although some has certainly been made with other instruments and the range of tools and materials now available is far wider than ever before. The book therefore shows in an accessible form a wide variety of works in different media and reveals some of the present preoccupations of a number of lettering artists, their models and modes of expression. The book will provide both enjoyment, and information and, perhaps, inspiration, for although the student will always derive encouragement from contemporary work it should be pointed out that the artists themselves may have used an extensive and varied range of models, from the past as well as the present. The secret behind much of the best work lies not so much on 'how can I do something' but rather on 'what do the words demand', 'what do I want to do' and only then 'how can I do it'. The work in this book will allow you to see something of the recent results of this process and show you that lettering can be an art as well as a craft, its applications as versatile and as variable as the mood or needs and the skill of the artist dictate.

Michael Gullick and Ieuan Rees, 1980

Calligraphy and lettering

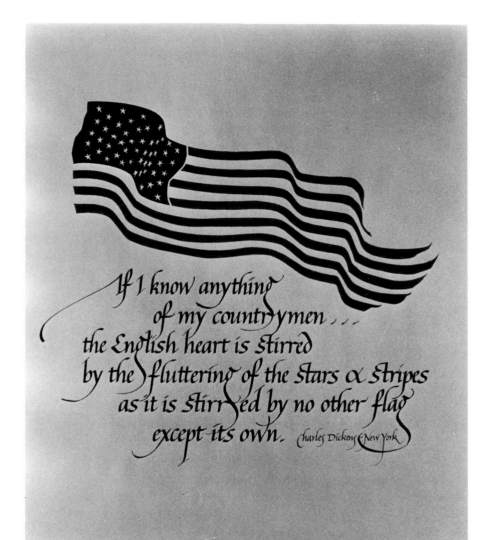

Stanley Knight
'Stars and Stripes'. Blue and red on white
paper. Original size 38 × 33 cm
(15 × 13 in).

Jean Evans
The Baker in *Hunting of the Snark*,
'Intimate Friends'. The large lettering is
written out in purple and silver
watercolour, the small lettering in
vermilion. All on tan paper.
Approximate size of original
20.3 × 61 cm (8 × 24 in).

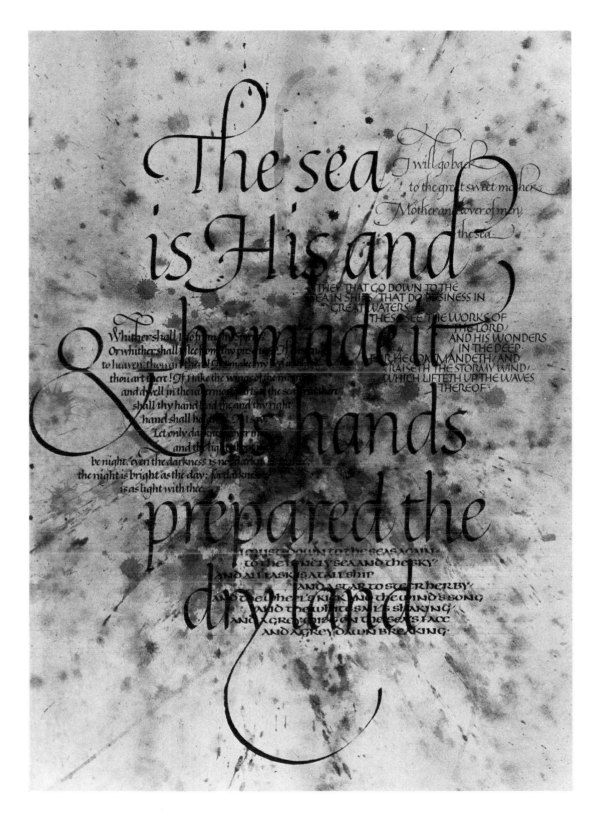

Charles Pearce
'The Sea'. Written out in coloured inks,
stick ink and gouache on handmade paper.

Villu Toots
Address to Valter Kraner. Original size
24.7 × 18 cm (9¾ × 7¼ in).

WE SHALL NOT cease from exploration
And the end of all our exploring
will be
to arrive where we started
& KNOW the place for the first time

Through the unknown,
remembered gate
When the last of earth left to discover
Is that
which was the beginning;

AT THE SOURCE of the longest river
The voice of the hidden waterfall
And the children in the apple tree
Not known,
because not looked for
But heard, half-heard, in the stillness
Between two waves of the sea.

QUICK NOW, HERE, NOW, ALWAYS—
A condition
of complete simplicity
[costing not less than everything]
And ALL SHALL BE WELL and

All manner of thing shall be well
When the tongues of flame are in-folded
Into the crowned knot of fire
And the fire and the rose are ONE.

from 'Four Quartets' by T S Eliot

Stanley Knight
Framed panel written in various shades of
green and blue on hand-made paper.
Original size 40.6 × 20.3 cm (16 × 8 in).

Jovica Veljovic
Lettering. Written out in ink with a
wooden stick on paper. Original size
19 × 38 cm (7½ × 15¼ in).

Jerry Kelly and Julian Waters
Quotation from the book of *Genesis*.
Written out in 23 carat shell gold on blue
Fabriano Roma paper. Original size
19 × 18.7 cm (7½ × 7⅜ in).

AND GOD
SAID·LET US
MAKE MAN IN
OUR IMAGE·
AFTER OUR
LIKENESS·

GENESIS

William Metzig
Quotation from Heraclitus. Written out
in watercolour and ink on paper. Original
size 36.8 × 27.9 cm (14¼ × 11 in).

The flowers fading like our hopes,
the leaves fading like our years,
the clouds fleeting like our illusions,
the light diminishing like our intelligence,
the sun growing colder like our affections,
the rivers becoming frozen like our lives,
all bear secret relations to our destinies.

Francois René De Chateaubriand — **A moral character is attached to autumnal scenes**

Marcy Robinson
Lettering written out in liquid stick ink
with a Speedball and William Mitchell
nibs. Original size 15.2 × 37 cm
($14\frac{5}{8}$ × 6 in).

Wendy Westover
Arms of the conservators of Wimbledon
and Putney Commons. Written out in
gouache, matt gold and India ink on grey
Ingres paper. Original size 30.4 × 25.4 cm
(12 × 10 in).

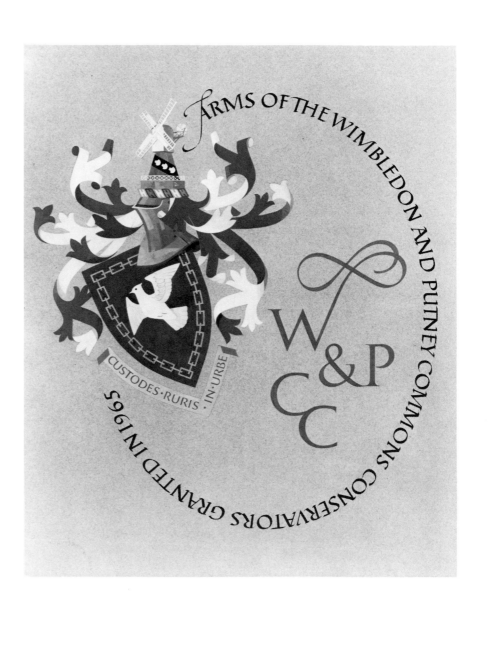

ARMS OF THE WIMBLEDON AND PUTNEY COMMONS CONSERVATORS GRANTED IN 1965

CUSTODES · RURIS · IN · URBE

W & P CC

¿En qué reino, en qué SONETO siglo, bajo qué silenciosa
Conjunción de los astros, en qué secreto día
Que el mármol no ha salvado, DEL VINO surgió la valerosa
Y singular idea de inventar la alegría?
Con otoños de oro la inventaron. El vino
Fluye rojo a lo largo de las generaciones
Como el río del tiempo y en el arduo camino
Nos prodiga su música, su fuego y sus leones.
En la noche del júbilo o en la jornada adversa
Exalta la alegría o mitiga el espanto
Y el ditirambo nuevo que este día le canto
Otrora lo cantaron el árabe y el persa.
Vino, enséñame el arte de ver mi propia historia
Como si ésta ya fuera ceniza en la memoria.

Jorge Luis Borges

Claude Dieterich
Soneto del Vino a poem by Jorge Luis
Borges. Black India ink on white
watercolour paper. A fountain pen was
used for the text and a steel pen for the
illustration. Overall width of lettering
43 cm (16¾ in).

Jovica Veljovic
'*Nihil difficile amanti puto*'. Original
size 15 × 22 cm (5⅞ × 8½ in).

Raphael Boguslav
Two highly decorative calligraphic
alphabets written out in ink on paper.
Original size 35.5 × 43 cm (14 × 17 in).

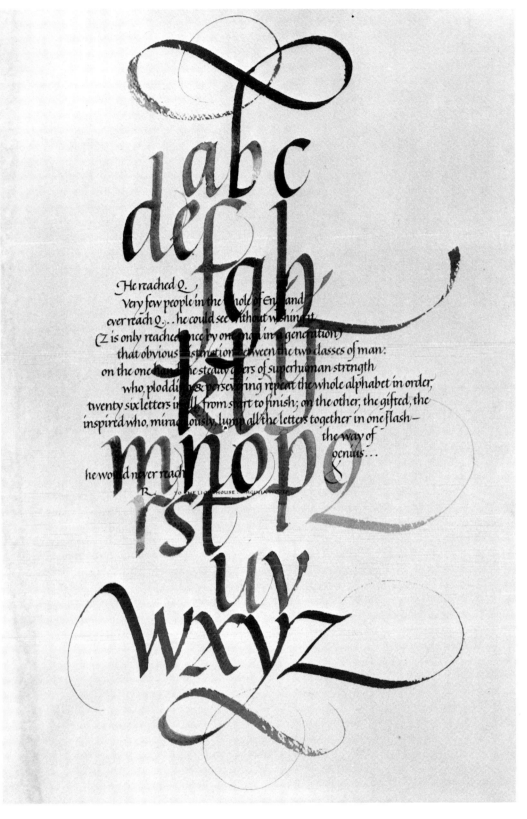

abc
de fgh
ij kl

He reached Q.
Very few people in the whole of England
ever reach Q... he could see without wishing it
(Z is only reached once by one man in a generation)
that obvious distinction between the two classes of man:
on the one hand the steady goers of superhuman strength
who, plodding & persevering repeat the whole alphabet in order,
twenty six letters in all, from start to finish; on the other, the gifted, the
inspired who, miraculously, lump all the letters together in one flash—
the way of
genius...

he would never reach R.

R.   TO THE LIGHTHOUSE   VIRGINIA WOOLF

mnopq
rst
uv
wxyz

Charles Pearce
Quotation from *To the lighthouse* by
Virginia Woolf. Written out in
watercolour on Strathmore watercolour
paper.

Claude Mediavilla
Calligraphy for Lure's Oath. Original size 32 × 50 cm (12¾ × 20 in).

Guillermo Rodriguez-Benitez
Quotation from Shakespeare's *The Merchant of Venice*, Act IV Sc I.

Alfred Linz
Quotation from Sigmund Graff. Overall width of original lettering 22.5 cm (9 in).

Raphael Boguslav
Clock with walnut frame and battery movement. Original size 48.4 × 48.4 cm (22 × 22 in).
Courtesy, Jon Henauer.

Stanley Knight
Christmas greetings.

Raphael Boguslav
'After many a summer dies the swan'.
Written out in black ink on white paper.
Original size 45.7 × 61 cm (18 × 24 in).

Alfred Linz
Quotation from Tolstoi. Overall width of
original lettering 15 cm (6 in).

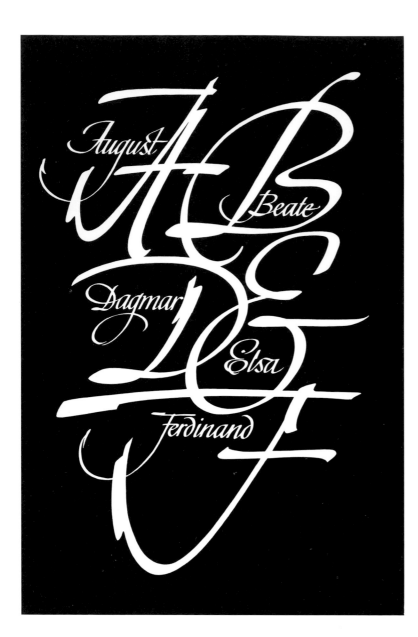

"The man
who has seen
the rising moon
break out
of the clouds at
midnight
has been present
like an
archangel at
the creation of
light and
of the world."
Ralph Waldo Emerson

Villu Toots
A sample page from a book of
Calligraphic Studies. Written out in white
gouache on indigo paper. Original size
23 × 15 cm (9 × 6 in).

James W McFarland
Quotation from Ralph Waldo Emerson.

Jean Evans
Alphabet.

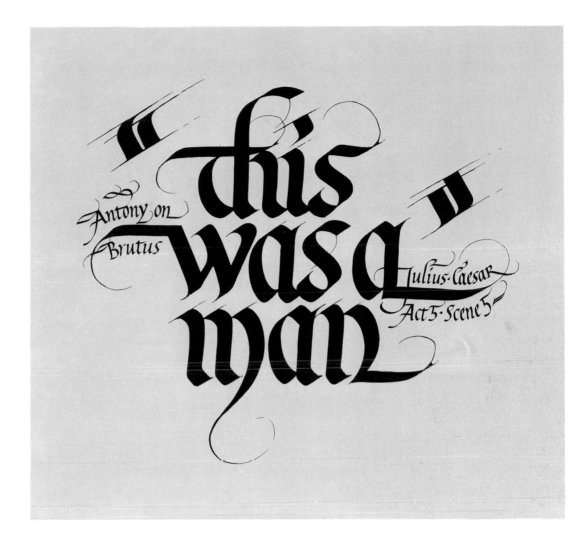

Ieuan Rees
Quotation from Shakespeare written out in black and sepia. Overall width of original lettering 16.5 cm (6½ in).

Patricia Weisberg
Lettering written out on Spunfelt paper. Original size 28 × 35.5 cm (11 × 14 in).

LOVE'S HERALDS
SHOULD BE THOUGHTS,
WHICH TEN ☙ Romeo & Juliet ☙
TIMES FASTER GLIDE
THAN THE SUN'S
BEAMS

Ieuan Rees
Demonstration piece done while Artist in Residence at Ysgol Eifionydd, Porthmadog, North Wales. Colour: vermilion.
Diameter of original 18.4 cm (7¼ in).

Paul Maurer
Lettering written in watercolour with metal pens. Original size 28 × 43 cm (11 × 17 in).

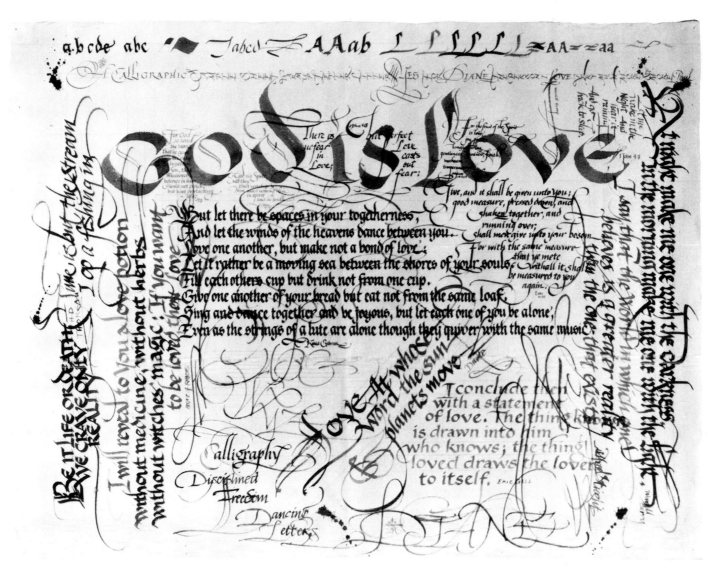

Paul Maurer
Lettering written in watercolour with metal pens and plastic quills. Original size 51 × 76.2 cm (20 × 30 in).

Jeanyee Wong
Two monograms.

*Viele Augenblicke
unvermischt
reinen Glückes verdanken
wir der Musik.
Sie läßt uns das Leben
losgelöst von allem
Stofflichen,
im Lichte idealer
Verklärung empfinden.*

HERMANN RITTER

Alfred Linz
Quotation from Hermann Ritter. Overall
width of original lettering 17 cm (6¾ in).

Jovica Veljovic
Lettering. Written out in ink with a
wooden stick on paper. Original size
20 × 28 cm (7¾ × 11 in).

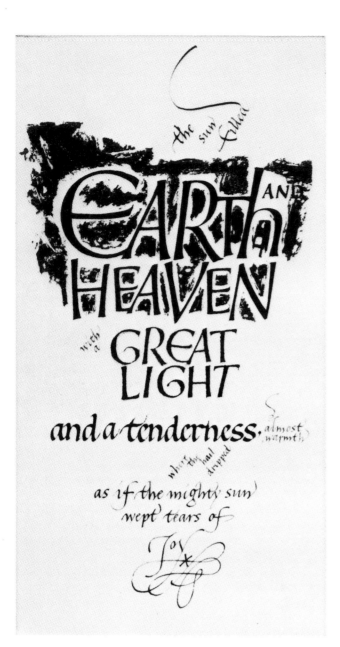

Ann Hechle
Quotation from *March* by Edward Thomas. An attempt to bring out the sound shapes of 'Earth and Heaven' and the intimate quality of the second half of the stanza. Written out in raised and burnished gold leaf and burnished gesso, blue and brown watercolour and stick ink with quills.

David Williams
1 *Corinthians*, Chapter 15, verses 51–52. Original size 53.5 × 17.7 cm (21 × 7 in).

BEHOLD I SHEW YOU A MYSTERY WE SHALL NOT ALL SLEEP BUT WE SHALL ALL BE CHANGED IN A MOMENT IN THE TWINKLING OF AN EYE AT THE LAST TRUMP FOR THE TRUMPET SHALL SOUND AND THE DEAD SHALL BE RAISED INCORRUPTIBLE AND WE SHALL BE CHANGED

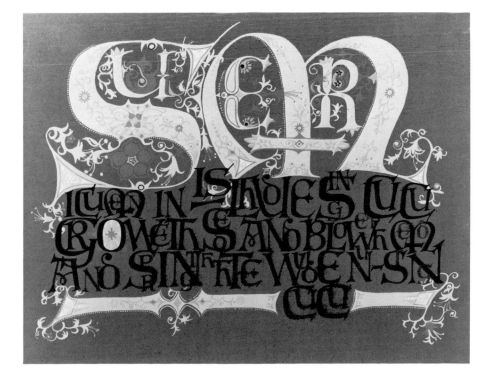

Ieuan Rees
Bilingual gilded vellum panel for 'The Hugh Owen Building' Aberystwyth. Original size 53.3 × 76.2 cm (21 × 30 in).

Hella Basu
Sumer. A thirteenth-century poem from *The Oxford Book of Verse*. Written out in gouache on charcoal paper. Original size 50.8 × 76.2 cm (20 × 30 in).

This is the day
which the Lord has made;
let us
rejoice
and
be glad
in it.

PSALM 118:24

Jeanyee Wong
Psalm 118 verse 24. Lettering written out in black ink on yellow paper. Overall width of lettering approximately 16 cm ($6\frac{1}{4}$ in).

I Morris
Quotation written out in orange and brown gouache on pale apricot ingres paper. Original size 29.2 × 43 cm ($11\frac{1}{2}$ × 17 in).

YOU CANNOT PROSPER BY DISCOURAGING THRIFT; QUOTATION BY

YOU CANNOT STRENGTHEN THE WEAK BY WEAKENING THE STRONG;

YOU CANNOT HELP THE POOR BY DESTROYING THE RICH; 1865

YOU CANNOT KEEP OUT OF TROUBLE BY SPENDING MORE THAN YOU EARN;

YOU CANNOT BUILD CHARACTER AND COURAGE BY TAKING AWAY

A MAN'S INITIATIVE AND INDEPENDENCE. ABRAHAM LINCOLN

Today is the first day of the rest of my life.

IEUAN REES

Ieuan Rees
Freely written quotation in black.
Approximate size of original 18 × 14 cm
(7 × 5½ in).

Ieuan Rees
Artwork. Originally gold-blocked on to a
leather bound book. Lettering actual size.

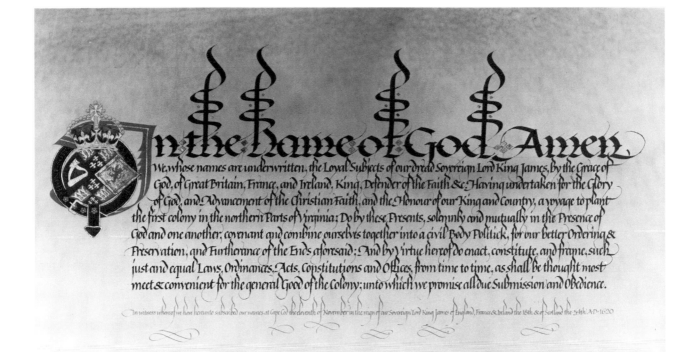

Charles Pearce
The Mayflower Compact. Gold leaf, ink and gouache on hand-made paper.
Original size 25.4 × 43 cm (10 × 17 in).

Patricia Weisberg
Quotation from Qadi Ahmad. Written out on Strathmore paper in coloured inks with Bouwsma pen and 2½ pt Mitchell nib. Letters in brown and green, quotation in brown and author's name in green.
Original size 35.5 × 43 cm (14 × 17 in).

THE WOODS DECAY,
THE WOODS DECAY AND FALL,
THE VAPOURS
WEEP THEIR BURDEN
TO THE GROUND,
MAN COMES & TILLS THE SOIL
AND LIES BENEATH,
AND AFTER MANY A SUMMER
DIES THE SWAN.

TENNYSON

John Prestianni
Quotation from *Tethonus* by A F
Tennyson. Brush lettering on vellum.
Original size 40 × 58.4 cm (16 × 23 in).

Facing page: 'The Scribe' by St Columba.
The writing is based on the Anglo-Saxon
styles of the 7th and 8th centuries AD.
Written out in ink and illuminated with
watercolour. Original size 76.2 × 53.3 cm
(30 × 21 in).

Bryan Winkworth
Poem *Manasija* by Vasko Popa. Written
out in black ink on white paper. Original
size 28 × 38 cm (11 × 5 in).

MANÁSIJA

VASKO POPA

Blue and gold
Last ring of the horizon
Last apple of the sun

OH ZOGRAF
HOW FAR DOES YOUR SIGHT REACH

DO YOU HEAR THE NIGHT HORSEMEN
Allah il ilallah

YOUR BRUSH DOES NOT TREMBLE
YOUR COLOURS ARE NOT AFRAID

THE NIGHT HORSEMEN COME CLOSER
Allah il ilallah

OH ZOGRAF
WHAT DO YOU SEE IN THE NIGHT'S DEPTH

Gold and blue
Last star in the soul
Last infinity in the eye

AN SCRÍOBAIDE

The Scribe · by Saint Columba, called Colum-cille·

Saint Columba, the great Irish missionary of the sixth century, founded the monastery of Iona off the coast of Scotland. He was born in 521 in the mountains of Donegal, and was baptised by the name Colum, which, in Latin, becomes Columba, or, "the dove." Later generations called him Columcille, or, "dove of the church." He had a great reputation as a scribe, so much so that later sources claim he transcribed more than three hundred copies of the gospels in his own hand. It is said that the Book of Durrow, probably written in the eighth century, was copied from a manuscript of Columba's hand.

He was highly educated and belonged to the learned order of Irish poets, the fild. As a result of his reputation as a poet, a number of poems of much later date have been attributed to him, such as the one transcribed here. In 561, while visiting his old master, Finbar of Moville, he clandestinely copied a a codex of the gospels for his own use. Upon discovering this, Finbar, to whom the book belonged, angrily brought the matter before the high king, demanding seizure of the copy. The king ruled against Columba, saying, "to every cow belongs her calf, & to every book its son book," establishing with this pronouncement, possibly for the first time, the law of copyright. According to accounts left us of his life, Columba, in vindication for the judgment that had been rendered against him, instigated the battle of Cul Dreimne, and many lives were lost.

As penance, Columba left Ireland, to "live in exile for Christ." In 563 he established the famous and influential monastery of Iona, where some people think the Book of Kells might have been written, late in the eighth century, from whence, conceivably, it might have been taken to Kells for safety before 806, when the monastery was sacked by Viking invasion. Ireland had only been converted to Christianity a little longer than a century when Columba founded his monastery on Iona. But from the first, Irish monasticism had embraced universal learning, that is, pagan and classical as well as Christian lore, unlike that of the Continent, which, until the beginning of the sixth century concerned itself primarily with learning which related to the spiritual side of monastic life. Ludwig Bieler, in IRELAND, HARBINGER OF THE MIDDLE AGES, says that

Is sith mo chrob on scríbainn;

ni organn mo gless geroll;

sceithid penn gulban caelta

óir, rodchda do dub glegorm.

Bruinnid srib n-ecna nodbairn

as mo laim degduinn desmais

doirtid a sreb por duillinn

do dub in chuilinn chiestglas.

Sinim mo phenn mbec mórthach

tar aenach lebar ligoll

cen scor fri selba segonn

dian scrib mo chrob on scríbainn.

My hand is tired from writing;
my sharp pen is not steady;
the pen, a slender beak, spouts
a dark stream of blue ink.
An unceasing stream of wisdom
pours from my brown hand.
It spills its flow of ink from the
blue-skinned holly over the page.
I send my wet little pen over a
whole pair of lovely books
Without ceasing for the wealth
of great ones, and so my
hand is tired from writing.

it was perfectly natural that the Irish, having become Christians, should be as appreciative of the new learning as they had been of their own traditional lore. This attitude is characteristic of Irish monasticism. The great respect which the Irish had for the written word is manifested most impressively by the fact that they developed a style of handwriting all their own, a national script."

The Irish, or insular, half-uncial as we know it today is regarded as being a development of scripts from antiquity, most likely of a continental half-uncial variety, which were brought to Ireland by the earliest missionaries. The Irish & later Anglo-Saxon hands differed in this respect from Continental hands of this period, primary examples of which are the Merovingian, Visigothic, & Beneventan scripts, as these are thought to have been attempts to formalize a mixture of half-uncial and local cursive hands. Bieler says: "Of all the numerous types of Latin script which came into existence during the early middle ages, the Irish script had the longest life and the widest dissemination. All the other ancient national scripts of Europe had to give way to the superior qualities of clarity and practicability of the Caroline minuscule. Even when, with the conquerors and the Continental religious orders, Romanesque and Gothic hands had come into use, the ancient Irish script continued to be employed for the writing of texts in the Irish language, and is so employed to this day."

Perhaps many of the great manuscripts of the seventh & eighth centuries perished in the sweep of Viking invasions which in the ninth century obliterated the Celtic civilization of Northumbria. In looting the rich and important monasteries, the invaders carried off the highly elaborate codices which were frequently decorated & lavishly covered with precious metals & jewels. Among very few others which have been preserved, the Lindisfarne Gospels, the Book of Kells, and the Book of Durrow stand out as masterpieces of scribal art. The motifs and images of the pagan Irish and Anglo-Saxon cultures, established and developed in metalwork and stone carving, were translated by Christian influence into the illumination adorning these books. For us, they are indeed a testament to the vision of their scribes.

Written and designed by John Prestianni, Winter 1979

Douglas C. McMurtrie:
We use the letters
of our alphabet every day
with the utmost ease and unconcern,
taking them almost
as much for granted
as the air we breathe.

We do not realize that each
of these letters is at our service today
only as the result of a long
and laboriously slow process of evolution
in the age-old art
of writing.

Le plus grand chef d'œuvre
de la littérature
n'est jamais qu'un alphabet
en desordre. Jean Cocteau

Das größefte
ift das Alphabet,
denn alle Weisheit fteckt darin.
Aber nur der erkennt den Sinn, der's recht
zusammenzusetzen
versteht.
Emanuel Geibel

Ἀρχὴ μεγίστη τοῦ βίου
τὰ γράμματα.

Hermann Zapf
Alphabet with quotations. Commissioned
by Philip Hofer. The Houghton Library,
Cambridge, Massachusetts.

Joan Pilsbury
October by Edward Thomas. Written
out in black, green and burnished gold on
vellum. Green and gold title. Double page
size 30.4 × 35.5 cm (12 × 14 in).

OCTOBER
Edward Thomas.

he green elm with the one great bough of gold
L ets leaves into the grass slip, one by one,—
T he short hill grass, the mushrooms small, milk-white
H arebell and scabious and tormentil,
T hat blackberry and gorse, in dew and sun,
B ow down to; and the wind travels too light
T o shake the fallen birch leaves from the fern;
T he gossamers wander at their own will.
A t heavier steps than birds' the squirrels scold.
T he rich scene has grown fresh again and new
A s Spring and to the touch is not more cool
T han it is warm to the gaze; and now I might
A s happy be as earth is beautiful,
W ere I some other or with earth could turn
I n alternation of violet and rose,
H arebell and snowdrop, at their season due,
A nd gorse that has no time not to be gay.
B ut if this be not happiness,—who knows?
S ome day I shall think this a happy day,
A nd this mood by the name of melancholy
S hall no more blackened and obscured be.

MIHI CREDE
RES SEVERA
Glaube mir,
eine ernste Sache ist eine
wahre Freude
EST
VERUM
GAUDIUM

SENECA

Rhythm is in harmony with nature and exists with manifold efficacy and form within all living creatures and within the phenomena of movement which surround us-in the regularity of our heart and pulse beats, in our breathing, or in the repetition of forms with like effects in plants of the same kind everywhere we feel the rhythmical law of renewal. As a temporary phenomenon of a rule, in continuous change, we recognise lettering also as rhythmical form.

The flowing movement in writing may be compared to the undulation of waves of water. When we observe waves with their stronger and weaker oscillations, we have a full rhythmical experience. The observation of this movement can give us the completed film, but the single photograph showing only the rigid fragment of one event can never do so. So it is with writing: the writer has the rhythmical experience whilst the beholder of the written matter can only guess at the vivacity of the letter strokes. An attempt to draw the movement of the wave results in the wavy line. By circumscribing the up and down movement of the mountains and valleys of the waves we get the rhythmical experience. But if we draw in such a way that the mountains and valleys in the waves harmonise exactly in their reversed form, then the vivid impulse of the movement is destroyed, and is replaced by a mechanical form.

These explanations as to the nature of rhythm clearly illustrate the immense value of the hand-written letter as against the designed form, for no designed form or type-set line can bear comparison in rhythmical strength with the aspect of the written line. Though, to be sure, we notice in type-set letters a certain harmonious effect, given by the proportional balance of spaces, yet the rigid repetitive effect of absolutely equal characters cannot give to the whole appearance the liveliness of rhythmical undulations. Just as in the fine arts, spontaneity appeals to us more strongly than the composition which is deliberately constructed, so lettering written freely with feeling takes precedence over any designed form of lettering.

WALTER KÄCH - RHYTHM IN LETTERING

Werner Schneider
Two pieces of calligraphy on Fabriano
paper. Original size 48.2 × 66 cm
(19½ × 26 in).

Arthur Baker
From a manuscript book of calligraphic alphabets and designs. Written out in ink with a coit pen on paper. Original size 61 × 96.5 cm (24 × 38 in).

O cunning enemy that to catch a saint with saints dost bait thy hook.

Angelo in Measure for Measure, act 2, scene 2

Nancy Culmone
Lettering written out in ink with a William Mitchell and automatic pen on paper. Overall width of lettering in original 18.5 cm (7¼ in).

John Woodcock
Brush drawn alphabet. Coloured inks and resist on handmade paper. Approximate size of original 38 × 51 cm (15 × 20 in).

Paul Freeman
Alphabet written out in Sumi red and black ink on Museum board with 1 inch brass nib and 1 inch wooden nib. Original size 81.2 × 45.7 cm (32 × 18 in).

Nancy Culmone
Lettering written in ink with a Speedball
pen on paper.

Love makes time pass

Time makes love pass

Ward Dunham
A gift to Richard Harrison in celebration
of his 70th birthday. Written in Chinese
ink with a 5 mm Brause nib on Butcher
paper.

Robert Boyajian
Freely written alphabet. Written out in
sepia and black India ink mixed, with
Lozada brass pen on Hammermill Bond.
Original size 43 × 35.5 cm (17 × 14 in).

Arthur Baker
Three pen manipulated alphabets.

Oigo decir que los amantes del vino serán condenados. No hay verdades comprobadas, pero hay mentiras evidentes. Si los amantes del vino y del amor van al Infierno, vacío debe estar el Paraíso.

Omar Khayyam

Claude Dieterich
A poem by Omar Khayyam. The initial was written in red India ink with reed. The text in black India ink with fountain pen. Overall width of lettering 52.7 cm (20½ in).

Jerry Kelly
Passage from the *Anatomy of Destructiveness* by Erich Fromm. Written out in blue and red watercolour, asterisks in black, on Honeysuckle Canson Mitentes paper. Original size 43 × 35.5 cm (17 × 14 in).

Erich Fromm * Today, when almost everything is made by machines, we notice little pleasure in skill except perhaps the pleasure people experience with hobbies like carpentry or the fascination of the average person when he can watch a goldsmith or weaver at his work; perhaps the fascination with a performing violinist is not only caused by the beauty of the music he produces but by the display of his skill * from 'the anatomy of human destructiveness' 1973

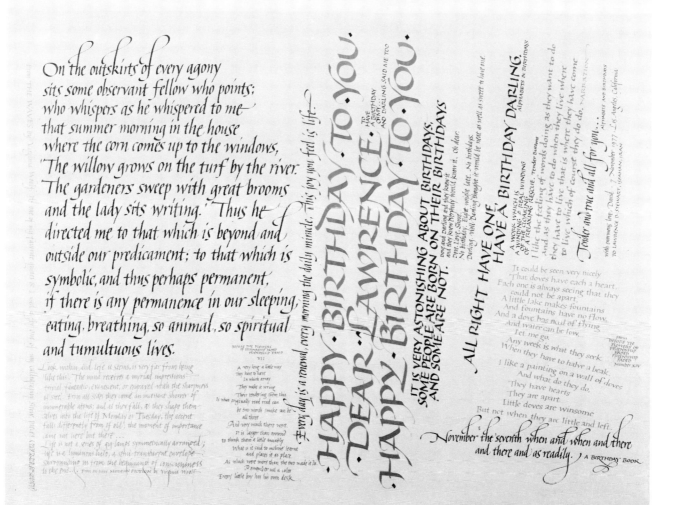

David Mekelburg
A spontaneous unplanned birthday greeting composed of quotations from the works of Gertrude Stein and Virginia Woolf. Written out on Bodleian mould-made paper in black Chinese stick ink, vermilion Japanese Sumi ink, and light blue and dark green gouache, with Brause nibs and turkey quills. Original size 52 × 71 cm (20½ × 28 in).

Nancy Winters
The Daffodils by William Wordsworth. Original size 25.5 × 47 cm (10 × 16 in).

IT IS FORTUNE NOT WISDOM THAT RULES A MAN'S LIFE
CICERO

Stuart Barrie
Quotation from Cicero. Original size framed 38 × 25.4 cm (15 × 10 in).

Anne Benedict
Quotation from W B Yeats. Original size 24 × 18.7 cm (9½ × 7⅜ in).

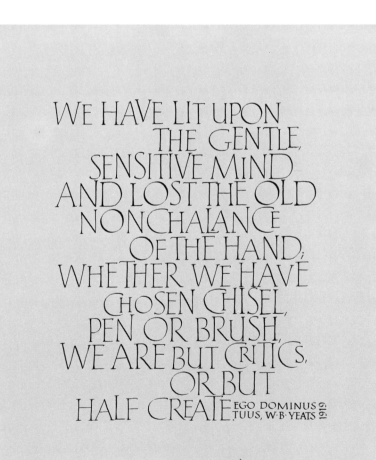

WE HAVE LIT UPON
THE GENTLE,
SENSITIVE MIND
AND LOST THE OLD
NONCHALANCE
OF THE HAND,
WHETHER WE HAVE
CHOSEN CHISEL,
PEN OR BRUSH,
WE ARE BUT CRITICS,
OR BUT
HALF CREATE EGO DOMINUS
TUUS, W·B·YEATS 1919

RUDOLF KOCH

The following excerpt was written by Fritz Kredel, one
of Koch's finest students. Koch and Kredel collaborated
on many projects in the Offenbach Workshop. This
paragraph is from the introduction to the 1976 reprint
of Das ABC Büchlein by Koch.

* The symbol Koch used   in his Offenbach Workshop

Koch's desire to be an educator was paramount. He
wrote a friend "I am nothing but an educator. Of course,
I do not want to educate calligraphers, but human
beings." The human relationship was more important to him
than the work. His first concern was helping his students
to improve themselves, to realize their greatest
potentials. To achieve this, he realized he must set an example,
and for that he was totally qualified. His reliability
and loyalty were irreproachable, his character was
noble. In financial matters a handshake or a verbal agreement was all that was ever necessary. ¶ He was
what I call a real man!

Jerry Kelly
Excerpt from the introduction to the 1976
reprint of *DAS ABC Büchlein* by Rudolf
Koch.

This question is one that only a very old man asks. My benefactor told me about it once when I was young, and my blood was too vigorous for me to understand it. Now I do understand it. I will tell you what it is: Does this path have a heart? All paths are the same: they lead nowhere. They are paths going through the bush, or into the bush. In my own life I could say I have traversed long, long paths, but I am not anywhere. My benefactor's question has meaning now. Does this path have a heart? If it does, the path is good; if it doesn't, it is of no use. Both paths lead nowhere; but one has a heart, the other doesn't. One makes for a joyful journey; as long as you follow it, you are one with it. The other will make you curse your life. One makes you strong; the other weakens you.

FOR ME
THERE IS ONLY
THE TRAVELING
ON PATHS
THAT HAVE
HEART,
ON ANY PATH
THAT MAY
HAVE HEART.
THERE
I TRAVEL AND
THE ONLY
WORTHWHILE
CHALLENGE
IS TO TRAVERSE
ITS FULL LENGTH.
AND THERE
I TRAVEL
LOOKING,
LOOKING
BREATHLESSLY.

*CARLOS CASTANEDA:
The Teachings of Don Juan
Written out by David Mekelburg
for Neene Billawala*

David Mekelburg
A passage from *The Teachings of Don Juan* by Carlos Castaneda. Written out with Brause nibs on BFK Rives paper. The small italic writing was done in black Chinese stick ink, the large capitals in Indian red designer's gouache, and the credit lines in grey designer's gouache. Original size 66 × 51 cm (26 × 20 in).

Donald Jackson
Presentation panel to commemorate the public service of Teodoro Moscoso. Written out on vellum in stick ink and pigments, with gesso, gum ammoniac and powder gilding with quills. Original size 66 × 51 cm (26 × 20 in).
Courtesy, Teodoro Moscoso.

Peter Halliday
Poem 43 from a collection of 73 Poems by
E E Cummings. Brush-painted in
watercolour on black, light and dark blue
and grey paper with a double-sided
reflecting strip down the centre. Original
size (within frame) 15.2 × 30.4 cm
(6 × 12 in).
*Reproduced by permission of the agent for the
late E E Cummings.*

Jean Evans
Lettering. Approximate size of original
40.6 × 51 cm (16 × 20 in).

Within the artwork, the following calligraphic text appears:

AND I TURNED TO SEE THE VOICE THAT SPAKE TO ME

AND IN THE MIDST OF THE SEVEN CANDLESTICKS ONE LIKE UNTO THE SON OF MAN AND HE HAD IN HIS RIGHT HAND SEVEN STARS AND HIS COUNTENANCE WAS AS was as the sun shineth in his

I am Alpha and Omega the first and the last & WHAT YOU SEE, WRITE IN A BOOK

AND GOD CALLED THE DRY LAND EARTH: AND THE GATHERING TOGETHER OF WATERS CALLED HE SEAS

Donald Jackson
Detail from 'I am the Alpha and Omega'. Written out in stick ink, gesso, gum ammoniac, shell gilding and gouache on vellum with quill and sponge. Height of original 33 cm (13 in).

Overleaf
Alison Urwick
Centre pages of a manuscript book presented to Heather Child in 1977 by The Society of Scribes & Illuminators. Written out in green, fawn and powdered gold capitals on india paper. Hand bound in vellum with silk ties, polished stones and silver thread. Actual size.

BRINGS
PERFECT
PEACE; COLOUR HAS SETTLED
ON EVERY·HILL,
HAZE ON THE LAKE
OF FULL WATER·

...G OF THE WILD ELM (THAT SERVES WELL THE BOWYERS)
& THE RESISTANT LIMBS DERWEN EVEN
OF THE TOUGH, KNARLED OAK TREE·

...RS LOW IN THE DEEPS OF THE VALLEY·WOOD THE FRAGILE BLODYN·Y· GWYNT
...THE ENCLOSURES BRIGHT·WITH THE FLOWER OF THE WIND·
...D·SORREL OF THE HOLLOWS, BY THE PLEASANT MARSHES
WHERE THE HINDS OFTEN COME·

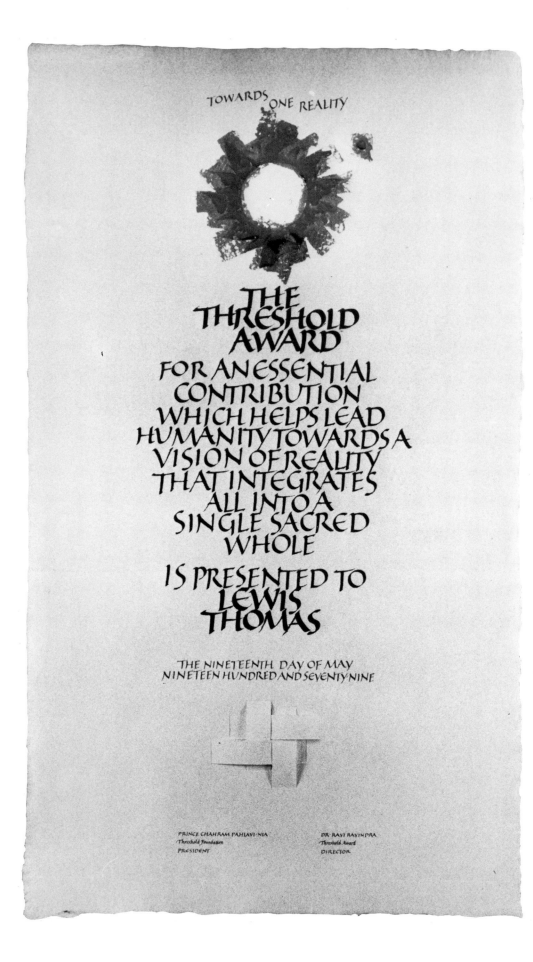

TOWARDS ONE REALITY

THE
THRESHOLD
AWARD
FOR AN ESSENTIAL
CONTRIBUTION
WHICH HELPS LEAD
HUMANITY TOWARDS A
VISION OF REALITY
THAT INTEGRATES
ALL INTO A
SINGLE SACRED
WHOLE

IS PRESENTED TO
LEWIS
THOMAS

THE NINETEENTH DAY OF MAY
NINETEEN HUNDRED AND SEVENTY NINE

PRINCE CHAHRAM PAHLAVI-NIA   DR· RAVI RAVINDRA
Threshold Foundation   Threshold Award
PRESIDENT   DIRECTOR

Stanley Knight
Text page of St John's Gospel written in Greek uncials on vellum. The writing in blue and black ink and raised gold. Original size 17.7 × 25.4 cm (7 × 10 in).

Cara Goldberg Marks
Wedding contract. Written out in ink and watercolour. Collection Tzipporan Brandes, Hong Kong.

Facing page
Donald Jackson
'The Threshold Award'. A presentation certificate written out in raised gold and black ink on paper. Original size 50 × 28 cm (19¾ × 11 in).

Colleen
Graffiti on a wall in Chicago 1971.
Original size 63.7 × 101.6 cm
(26 × 40 in).

Jovica Veljovic
Decorative lettering.
Written in ink with a wooden stick on paper.
Original size 11.5 × 17 cm ($4\frac{3}{4} \times 6\frac{7}{8}$ in).

Villu Toots
'Ann'. Experimental page of letters in
brown, red and orange. Original size
38.5 × 28 cm (15 × 11 in).

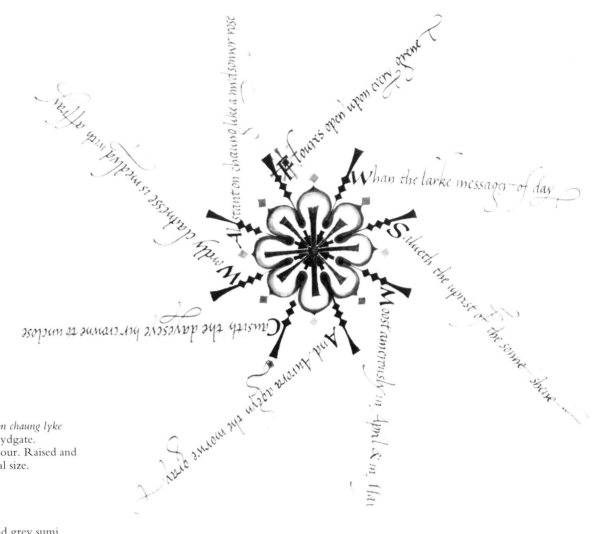

Ann Hechle
Quotation from *Al stant on chaung lyke a mydsomyr rose* by John Lydgate. Brown and pink watercolour. Raised and burnished gold leaf. Actual size.

Jean Evans
'The Centipede'. Black and grey sumi stick ink and gold watercolour on watercolour paper. Approximate size of original 75 × 250 cm (30 × 10 in).

BUTINTHE *Art* OF *Calligraphy*

ASINALLARTSTHEIDEAINTHEMI
NDISTHEULTIMATEYARDSTICK
BYWHICHWEEVALUATEMERITIN
THEART·PRODUCT·THETECHNIC
ALPRE-REQUISITES-TOOLSMAT
ERIALSANDMETHODOFWORK
ING-THOUGHNEEDEDAREALW
AYSSUBORDINATETOTHEIRME
NTALEXEMPLAR·TECHNIQUEIS
ONLYAMEANS·SKILLFULLYWRO
UGHTEXPRESSIONSOFINCONSE
QUENTIALIDEASAREMORELIKE
LYTOAROUSEDISMAYTHANAD
MIRATION·POORLYWRITTENLE
TTERSSKILLFULLYCHISELLEDARE
ALWAYSUGLIERTHANWELL-WRI
TTENLETTERSPOORLYCUTSINCE
ADEFECTINTHEMEANSISLESSDA
MAGINGTHANADEFECTINTHE
MENTALPATTERN FATHER CATICH

Jovica Veljovic
'But in the Art of Calligraphy . . .'
Original size 44 × 32.5 cm (17 × 12½ in).

63

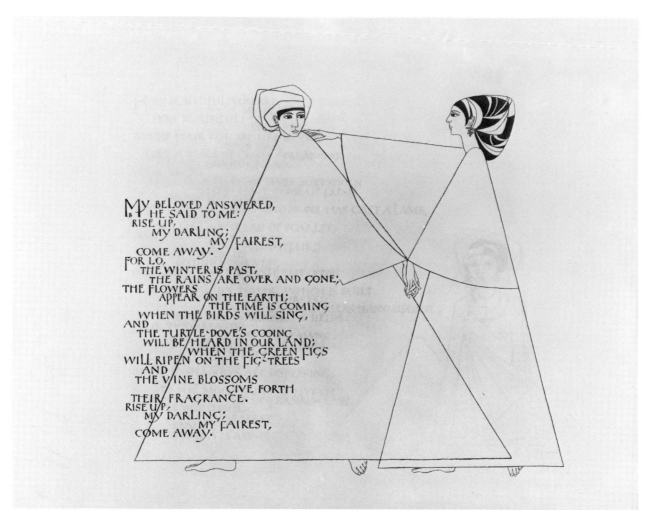

Alison Urwick
Extract from *The Song of Songs*. Written out in Chinese ink and watercolour with brush on hand-made paper. Original size 29.8 × 23.4 cm (11¾ × 9¼ in).

David Williams
Alphabet. Actual size.

FIELD POPPY

Summer set lip to earth's bosom bare

And left the flushed print of a poppy there

Like a YAWN OF FIRE from the grass it came,

And the fanning wind puffed it to flapping flame

Francis Thompson

Sheila Waters

Left: Title page lettering of *Under Milk Wood* by Dylan Thomas. Manuscript book commissioned by Edward Hornby Esq. Original size of lettering panel illustrated here 27.3 × 11.4 cm (10¾ × 4½ in). Overall page size 37.8 × 25.4 cm (14½ × 10 in).

Above: Field Poppy. Original size 17 × 9.3 cm (6⅝ × 3⅝ in).

Overleaf: Two pages from a manuscript book of *Under Milk Wood* by Dylan Thomas. Commissioned by Edward Hornby Esq. Original page size 37.8 × 25.4 cm (14½ × 10 in).

the roof of Handel Villa see the Women's
Welfare hoofing. bloomered, in the moon.

At the sea-end of town, Mr and Mrs Floyd,
the cocklers, are sleeping as quiet as death,
side by wrinkled side, toothless, salt and
brown, like two old kippers in a box.
And high above, in Salt Lake Farm, Mr Utah
Watkins counts, all night, the wife-faced
sheep as they leap the fences on the hill,
smiling and knitting and bleating just like
Mrs Utah Watkins.

Yawning	Thirty-four, thirty-five, thirty-six, forty-eight,	UTAH WATKINS
	eighty-nine...	
Bleating	Knit one slip one	MRS UTAH WATKINS
	Knit two together	
	Pass the slipstitch over...	

	Ocky Milkman, drowned asleep in Cockle	FIRST VOICE
	Street, is emptying his churns into the Dewi	
	River,	
Whispering	regardless of expense;	OCKY MILKMAN
	and weeping like a funeral.	FIRST VOICE
	Cherry Owen, next door, lifts a tankard to	SECOND VOICE
	his lips but nothing flows out of it. He shakes	
	the tankard. It turns into a fish. He drinks	
	the fish.	
	P. C. Attila Rees lumps out of bed, dead to	FIRST VOICE
	the dark and still foghorning, and drags out	
	his helmet from under the bed; but deep	

Softly. WHAT seas did you see,   ROSIE PROBERT
Tom Cat, Tom Cat,
In your sailoring days
Long long ago?
What sea beasts were
In the wavery green
When you were my master?

I'll tell you the truth.   CAPTAIN CAT
Seas barking like seals,
Blue seas and green,
Seas covered with eels
And mermen and whales.

What seas did you sail   ROSIE PROBERT
Old whaler when
On the blubbery waves
Between Frisco and Wales
You were my bosun?

As true as I'm here   CAPTAIN CAT
Dear you Tom Cat's tart
You landlubber Rosie
You cosy love
My easy as easy
My true sweetheart,
Seas green as a bean
Seas gliding with swans
In the seal-barking moon.

59

Peter Halliday
Vision and Prayer by Dylan Thomas from
The Poems published by J M Dent & Sons
Ltd and New Directions Inc. (Reproduced
by permission of the Trustees of the late
Dylan Thomas.) Original size
55.8 × 22.8 cm (21¾ × 8⅞ in).

Facing page
Charles Pearce
Declaration of Independence. Manuscript
book in a private collection. Written out
and decorated in gold and silver leaf and
gouache with pens and brushes on hand-
made paper. Original size 43 × 58.4 cm
(17 × 23 in).

Facing page
Donald Jackson
Letters Patent granting the Barony of
Charteris of Amisfield. Written out in
Chinese stick ink, gesso ammoniac and
powdered gilding with quills and brush.
Original size 41.9 × 55.8 cm
(16½ × 22 in).
Courtesy, Lord Charteris of Amisfield.

68

I hate Spiders I dislike all kinds of insects. Their cold intermitted industry repel me. Their empty, stereotyped unintelligence

&

I am not altogether happy about the future of the Human Race: when I think of the slow refrigeration of the Earth, the Sun's wandering and the ultimate, inevitable collapse of the Solar System, I have grave misgivings

St Clair Richard
Lettering written out in Sumi ink with reeds and quills on hand-made paper. Original size 38 × 30.4 cm (15 × 12 in).

Facing page
Kenneth Breese
The British Library Translation of the *Magna Carta*, part of the Bicentennial gift to the American People. Final version etched out and gilded on clear glass. Original size 41.8 × 24.2 cm (19 × 11 in).

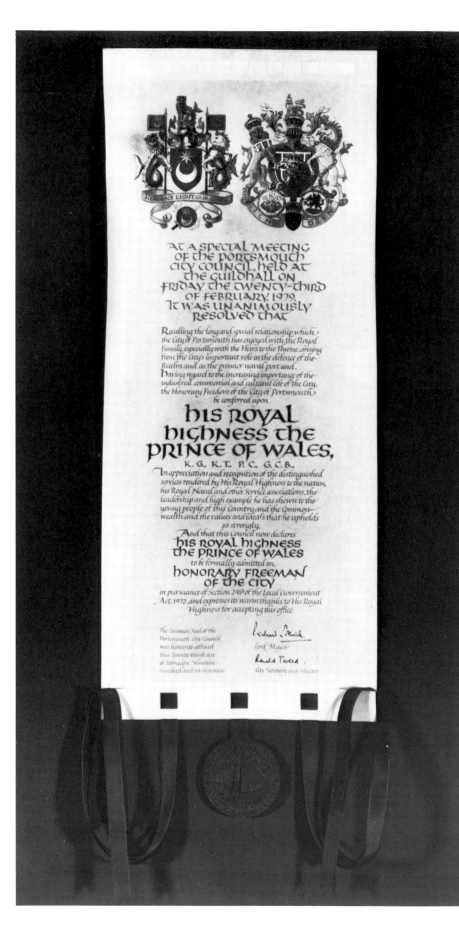

David Graham
Freedom Scroll presented by the City of
Portsmouth to HRH the Prince of Wales.
Main text in blue. Decorated with raised
and flat gold. Surface: Vellum. Original
size 58 × 23.5 cm (22½ × 9 in).
*By gracious permission of HRH the Prince of
Wales and courtesy of Portsmouth City Council.*

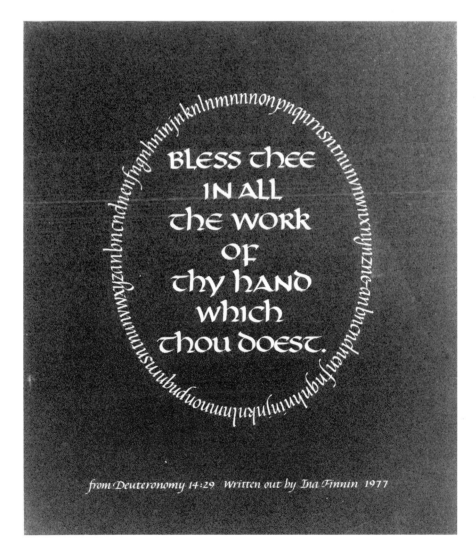

Donald Jackson
Presentation certificate written out in black stick ink and powder gold with quill pen on vellum. Original size 19 × 40.6 cm (7½ × 16 in).

Ina Saltz
Quotation from the book of *Deuteronomy*. Written out in gouache with Mitchell nibs on Canson paper. Original size 38.7 × 32.3 cm (15¼ × 12¾ in).

New York
City Ballet

John E Benson
Brush lettering. Brush and ink on Japanese
paper. Width of original 23.7 cm (9¼ in).

Linda Christensen
Lettering written out in frisket,
watercolour wash and gouache on
watercolour paper with Speedball nibs.

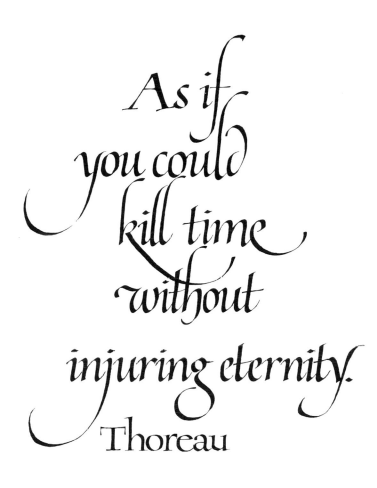

As if
you could
kill time
without
injuring eternity.
Thoreau

Sir Richard Howe
1680-1682

Paul Shaw
Quotation from Thoreau. Original size
28 × 21.5 cm (11 × 8¾ in).

Joan Pilsbury
Record of Arms of the Prime Wardens of
The Fishmonger's Company, Volume I.
Full colour and gold on vellum. Original
size 31.7 × 24 cm (12½ × 9½ in).

Vera Ibbett
Alphabet design. Diameter of original
16.8 cm (6 in).

PEOPLE DONT
REALIZE HOW
A MAN'S
WHOLE LIFE
CAN BE
CHANGED
BY
ONE BOOK

William Metzig
Quotation from Malcolm X. Written out
in inks on paper. Original size 36.8 ×
26 cm (14½ × 10¼ in).

Guillermo Rodriguez-Benitez
Letters cut from a heavy black paper and
mounted on white paper. Original size
28 × 19 cm (11 × 7½ in).

Maura Cooper Barnard
'Uncial design'. Exhibition piece for a
show at the Brooklyn Museum. Black
India ink on De Wint paper.
Original size 33 × 20 cm (13 × 8 in).

78

Werner Schneider
Lettering. Original size 58.5 × 37.5 cm
(23 × 15 in).

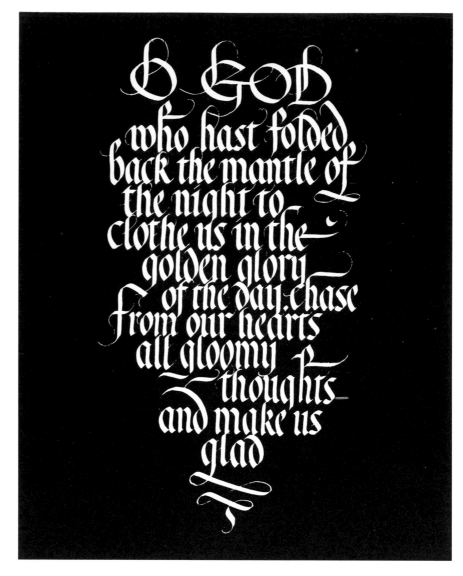

Dorothy Avery
Lettering in white gouache on black
paper. Approximate size of original
54 × 28.6 cm (7 × 13 in).

Margery Raisbeck
Lettering. Original size 13.9 × 20.2 cm
(5½ × 8 in).

Ward Dunham
'The' greatly enlarged.

JOHN CLARE AND WHAT IS LIFE? –
A mist retreating from the morning sun,
AN HOUR-GLASS
A busy, bustling, still repeated dream.
ON THE RUN,

Wendy Westover
Quotation from John Clare. Alternate
lines in brown and white. Brush and fine
pen lettering on Kraft paper. Original size
35.5 × 55.8 cm (14 × 22 in).

John Weber
Quotation from Mahatma Gandhi.
Commissioned by Joyce Miller of CARE,
an organization helping needy people
around the world. Original size
22.8 × 30.4 cm (9 × 12 in).

To the millions who have to
go without two meals a day
the only acceptable form in
which God dare appear is food.

MAHATMA GANDHI

In order that the foresaid injurious efforts of the king of England may the more conveniently be repressed and that the said king be the more quickly compelled to withdraw from his perverse and hostile incursions, the said king of Scots shall take care to begin and continue war against the king of England at his own cost and expense with all his power and with all the power of his subjects and of his kingdom, as often as it be opportune. The prelates of Scotland, as far as it be lawful to them, with the earls barons and other nobles and also the universitates ac communitates villarum of the kingdom of Scotland shall make war against the said king of England in the same manner as is above expressed, with all their strength. The prelates earls barons and other nobles and also the universitates communitatesque notabiles of the said kingdom of Scotland shall direct to us as soon as may be their letters patent hereon fortified with their seals. It was also agreed that if it happen the foresaid king of England to invade the kingdom of

Scotland by himself or by another after war has begun by the king of Scots at our request, or after this present agreement or treaty has been entered upon between us by occasion thereof, we provided we be forewarned thereof on the part of the same king of Scots within a suitable time, shall give him help by occupying the said king of England in other parts, so that he shall thus be distracted to other matters from the foresaid invasion which he has begun. If however, the foresaid king of England happens personally to leave England or goes out of it with a notable number of infantry or cavalry while war lasts between him and us, then especially the said king of Scotland with all his power shall take care to invade the land of England as widely or deeply as he can

George Thomson
'Treaty with France 1295'. Written out in
ink and watercolour with raised gilding
on hand-made paper. Original size
50 × 37 cm (19½ × 14⅜ in).

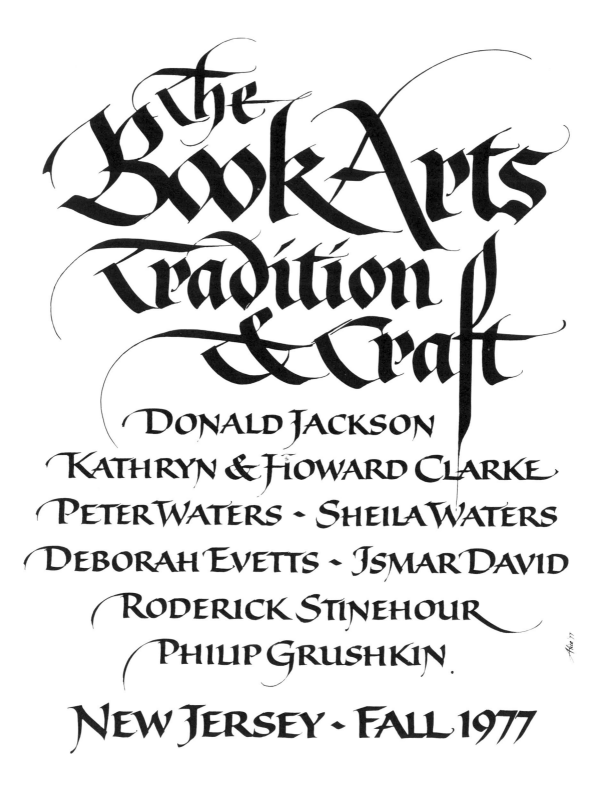

The Book Arts Tradition & Craft

DONALD JACKSON
KATHRYN & HOWARD CLARKE
PETER WATERS · SHEILA WATERS
DEBORAH EVETTS · ISMAR DAVID
RODERICK STINEHOUR
PHILIP GRUSHKIN

NEW JERSEY · FALL 1977

Alice
Poster. The original is an unretouched
piece for exhibition, later reproduced in
the same size as a poster for a lecture series.
Original size 59.6 × 47 cm (23½ × 18½ in).

For a long time it had seemed to me
that life was about to begin – real life.
But there was always some obstacle in the way.
Something to be got through first,
some unfinished business; time still to be served,
a debt to be paid. Then life would begin.
At last it dawned on me
that these obstacles were my life.

B. HOWLAND · Calligraphy by David Mekelburg

MY
HAND
IS TIRED
FROM
WRITING,
MY
SHARP
PEN
IS NOT
STEADY

sceithid penn-tulhan caelda
dig indaelda do dub glegorm.

Is scith mo chrob
on scribainn
in digainn mo tles tegoll;

the PEN,
A SLENDER
BEAK,
SPOUTS
A DARK
STREAM
OF
BLUE INK

SAINT COLUMBA
ALSO KNOWN AS
COLUMCILLE: GAELIC FOR
"DOVE OF THE CHURCH",
521–597 A.D.

the
SCRIBE

Bruinnid sruaimm n-ecna ndedairn
as mo láim deghduinn desmais;
doirtid a dig for duiblinn
do dub in chuilinn chnesglais

AN
UNCEASING
STREAM
OF WISDOM
POURS
FROM MY
BROWN
SHAPELY
HAND

IT
SPILLS ITS
FLOW OF INK
FROM THE
BLUE-SKINNED
HOLLY
OVER
THE PAGE

Sínim mo phenn
mbec mbraenach
za aenach lebar ligoll

I SEND
MY WET
LITTLE
PEN
OVER
A WHOLE
FAIR
OF LOVELY
BOOKS
WITHOUT
CEASING

FOR
THE WEALTH
OF GREAT
ONES
AND SO
MY
HAND
IS TIRED
FROM
WRITING

cen scor, fri selha segonn,
dian sci mo chrob
on scribonn.

David Mekelburg
A quotation from the book *Life in the Snakepit* by Bette Howland. Written out in Chinese stick ink with an automatic pen on Strathmore Kid Finish Bristol.

Terry O'Donnell
'The Scribe'. Written out in ink and gouache with a metal and nylon pen on Saunders hand-made paper. Original size 33 × 45 cm (13 × 17 in).

Theo Varlet # AN EDUCATION THROUGH BOOKS

is a companion which no misfortune
can depress — no crime destroy —
no enemy alienate, — no despotism
enslave.

* At home, a friend; abroad an
introduction; in solitude, a solace;
and in society an ornament.

Without books, what is man?

Hermann Zapf
Quotation by Theo Varlet.
Commissioned for The San Francisco
Public Library for their collection of
calligraphy.

Calligraphy and lettering for reproduction

Ivan
THE TERRIBLE
& Ivan THE FOOL

David Gatti
Lettering for a bookjacket. Width of
original artwork 29.6 cm ($11\frac{5}{8}$ in).

Pat Topping
Christmas greetings card. Printed size
14×14 cm ($5\frac{1}{2} \times 5\frac{1}{2}$ in).

Map labels (The Pendragon endpapers):

Irish Sea • North Sea • Glein Estuary • English Channel • Atlantic Ocean

IRELAND • WALES • VALENTIA • DYFID • DUMNONIA • MENAEVIA • CANTII • LYONESSE (CORNWALL) • LAND'S END

Yr Widdfa (Snowdon) • CARBONEK • Fortress of Deva • GWYNFID • Glevum (Gloucester) • Isca (Caerleon) • Corinium (Cirencester) • Badon • Verulamium (St. Albans) • Londinium R. (Thames) • Aquae Sulis (Bath) • Ynis Witrin (Glastonbury) • Calleva (Silchester) • Londinium (London) • Durnovernum (Canterbury) • Camelot (Cadbury) • Venta (Winchester) • Dunovaria (Dorchester) • Onna (Nursling) • Clausentium • Port Adurni (Portchester) • Novemagus (Chichester) • Anderita (Pevensey) • Cantii Coast • Blackwater • OUTLAND HILLS • Place of the Gathering • Fortress of Tintagel • Fortress of Dor • Villa of Ectorius • Coensia (Totnes) • Camlan (Slapton) • Venta (Caister) • ISLE OF WIGHT

Inset map: BRITAIN • DALRIADA • IRELAND • Silver Wood • Hadrian's Wall • VALENTIA • MENAEVIA • ARMORICA • Broceliande • Atlantic Ocean

Miles 0 25 50 • Kms. 0 50

N

A. Karl

Anita Karl
Endpapers for *The Pendragon* by Catherine Christian, published by Alfred Knopf. 1979.

David Mekelburg
Calligraphic letterheading.

Donald K. Adams

David Quay
Lettering for a bookjacket. Width of
original artwork 25.4 cm (10 in).

David Kindersley
Two bookplates. Actual printed size.

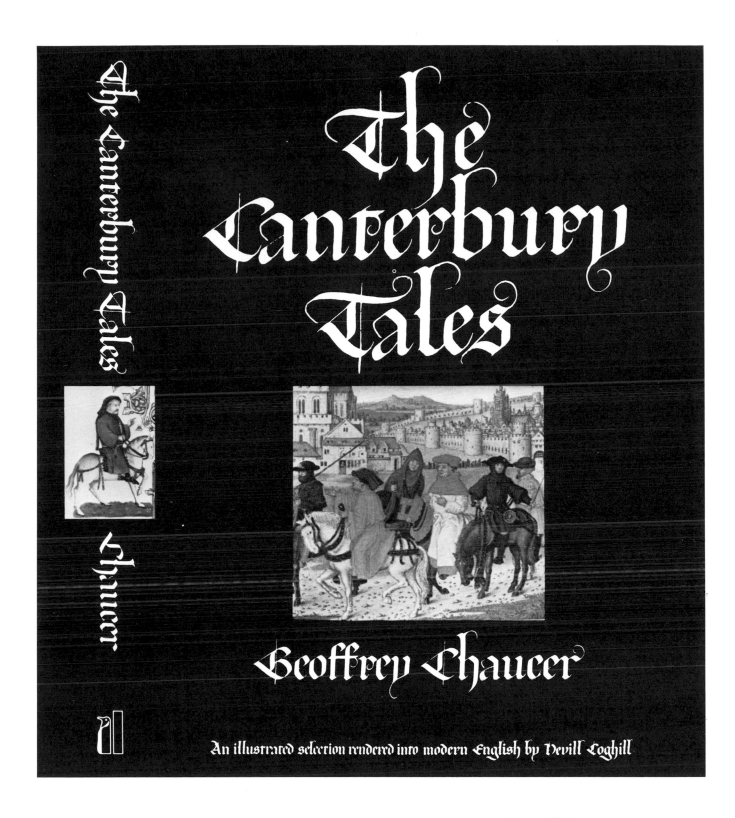

The Canterbury Tales

Geoffrey Chaucer

An illustrated selection rendered into modern English by Nevill Coghill

Nancy Winters
Calligraphy for *The Canterbury Tales* published in 1977 by Penguin. Shown here on the jacket but used throughout the book for titles and headings. Printed size 21 × 19 cm (8¼ × 7½ in).

Bo Berndal
Christmas greetings card. Original width of lettering 12.6 cm (4⅞ in).

Gerry Fleuss and Lida Lopes Cardozo
Bookplate. Actual printed size.

Kenneth Breese
Handpainted symbol for the Gordon Restaurant, Scotland.

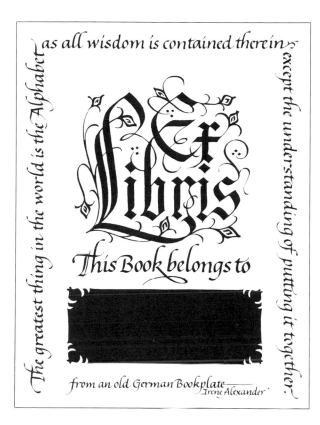

Irene Alexander
Bookplate designed for personal use and to raise money for the Society for Italic Handwriting British Columbia. Written out with William Mitchell round-hand nibs number 00, 3, 4 and 5. The name area, 'This book belongs to' and the surrounding lettering in red. All other lettering in black. Actual printed size. Original size 15.2 × 20.3 cm (6 × 8 in).

Muriel Nasser
Lettering for a bookjacket.

Donald Jackson
Press advertisement. Written out in stick ink with quill on layout paper. Original size 20.3 × 10 cm (8 × 4 in). Actual printed size. *Courtesy of the Craftwork Gallery.*

John Weber
Alphabet rosette used as a logotype on
John Weber's personal stationary.
Diameter of original 51 cm (20 in).

Bo Berndal
Two bookplates. Actual printed size.
Original width of lettering 'JB' 5.2 cm
(2 in). Original width of oval 'Peo
Kjellgren' 9 cm (3½ in).

DAS AUSLÄUTEN

In meiner Heimat lebt der Brauch:
ist verronnen der Weihe-Rauch,
liegt der Tote im Grabe,
klumpt auf den Sarg die Schollengabe,
so tönen auf einmal alle Glocken·
Und blieb ein Seelefünklein wo hocken,
ein Atem bloß, ein Seufzer, der bang
vorm Tode in die Büsche entsprang:

die Glocken ernten alles ein,
ihr Echo betet in Dickicht und Hain,
sie beschreien den Acker, besingen den Hang
mit erzenem Munde, mit der Ewigkeit Klang!

Sie schwellen ums Haus, verjagen den Alb,
sie schlucken noch der Dinge Hauch,
sie drängen den Toten von Roß und Kalb,
zerren zuletzt ihn vom Hunde auch·

Richard Billinger

Herbstbeginn

Der Hirte singt zum Abendstern·
Im Apfel bräunet sich der Kern·
Wipfelmüd die Bäume schweigen·
Nebel in die Wiesen steigen·
Beere sich an Beere hängt·
Zur Aster sich die Hummel drängt·
Der Kern aus reifer Pflaume quoll·
Ein Birnlein in der Faust mir schwoll·
Ich sauge mich ins Fruchtfleisch ein,
die Wange heiß vom ersten Wein·

Richard Billinger

Friedrich Neugebauer
Two pieces from *Der Garten Haucht* by
Richard Billinger. Printed size
28.5 × 12.8 cm (11¼ × 5 in).

FOR
UNTO US
A CHILD
IS BORN,
UNTO US
A SON
IS GIVEN:
AND HE
SHALL BE
CALLED
THE PRINCE
OF PEACE

GLORIA INALTISSIMIS DEO ET IN TERRA PAX HOMINIBUS BONAE VOLUNTATIS

John Prestianni
Christmas greetings card. Actual printed size.

John Smith
Book mark. Actual printed size.

IF MAN IS MODERATE AND CONTENTED
THEN EVEN AGE IS NO BURDEN
IF HE IS NOT
THEN EVEN YOUTH IS
FULL OF CARES

PLATO

Ismar David
One of a set of seventeen style examples
from the Geyer Studio writing book, *Our
Calligraphic Heritage*. Printed size
18×21.6 cm ($7 \times 8\frac{7}{8}$ in).

Ieuan Rees
Letterheading. Actual printed size.

A cynic is one
who knows the price
of everything
and the value
of nothing

oscar wilde.

Ismar David
One of a set of seventeen style examples
from the Geyer Studio writing book, *Our
Calligraphic Heritage*. Printed size
18 × 21.6 cm (7 × 8⅞ in).

Marie Angel
Left: Decorative initial from *Bird, Beast
and Flower*. A book of poems to be
published in 1980 by Chatto and Windus
Limited, London.

Right: Decorative initial from *Tucky the
Hunter* by James Dickey. Illustrated by
Marie Angel, published in 1978 by Crown
Publishers Inc., New York.

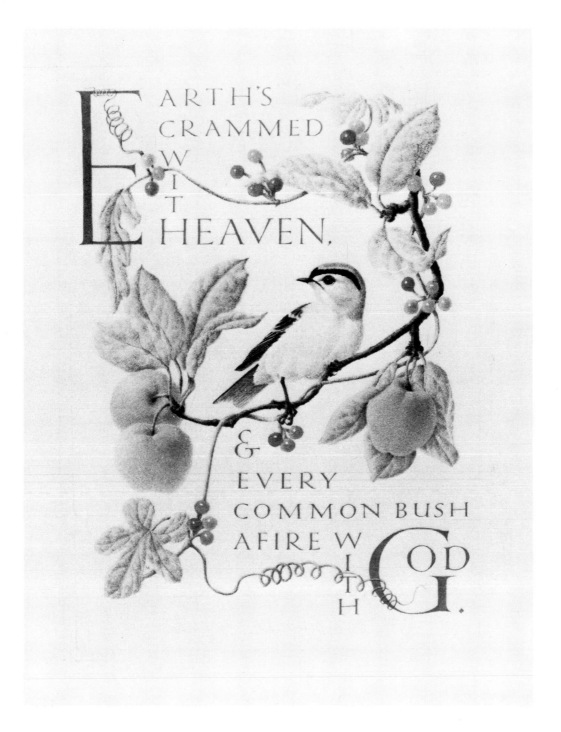

EARTH'S CRAMMED WITH HEAVEN, & EVERY COMMON BUSH AFIRE WITH GOD.

Marie Angel
Quotation from *Aurora Leigh* by Elizabeth Barrett Browning. One of twelve drawings for a calendar, published in 1979 by the Green Tiger Press, La Jolla, California.

Villu Toots
Decorative initial. Written and illuminated with a quill. Original size 14.5 × 12.3 cm (5¾ × 5 in).

Villu Toots
Two bookplates. Actual printed size.

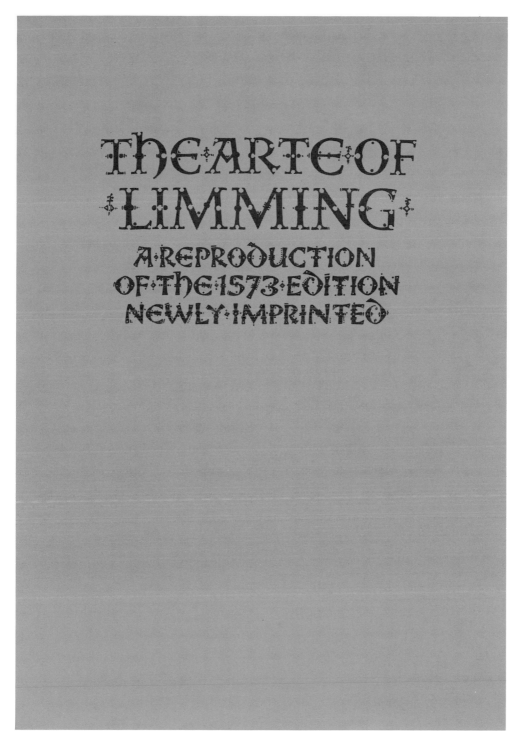

Michael Gullick
Front cover to *The Art of Limming*
published by the Society of Scribes and
Illuminators, London, 1979. Actual
printed size.

If a job's worth doing it's probably in the Headhunter

The Daily Telegraph
Appointments Pages

Nancy Winters
Poster for *The Daily Telegraph.*
Reproduced for display on station
hoardings. Printed size 152 × 102 cm
(59¼ × 39¾ in).

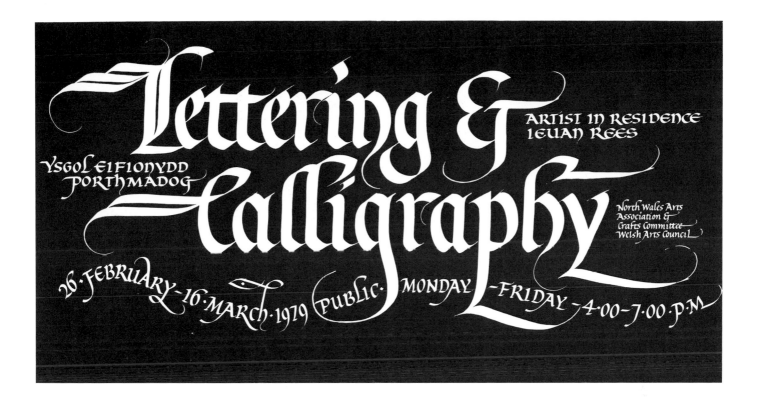

Ieuan Rees
Poster design. White on olive green.
Printed size 21.5 × 40.6 cm (8½ × 16 in).

James Hayes
Calligraphy for the Pentalic–Taplinger
Calendar 1980. Printed size
21.5 × 21.5 cm (8½ × 8½ in).

Ieuan Rees
Design for brochure and poster. Later to be incorporated in the facia of the Dylan Thomas Theatre. White letters reversed out of dark brown. Brochure size 14.7 × 19 cm (5⅞ × 7½ in).

Peter Halliday
Christmas greetings card. Original size 16.5 × 21 cm (6½ × 8¼ in). Printed size 8.2 × 10.4 cm (3¼ × 4½ in).

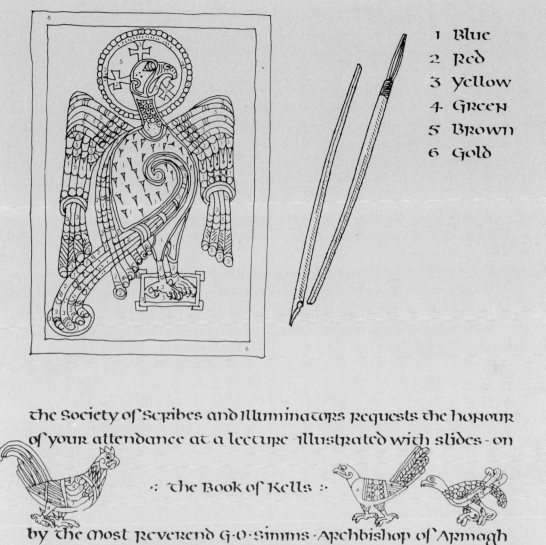

1 Blue
2 Red
3 Yellow
4 Green
5 Brown
6 Gold

the Society of Scribes and Illuminators requests the honour
of your attendance at a lecture · illustrated with slides · on

:· the Book of Kells ·:

by the Most Reverend G·O·Simms · Archbishop of Armagh
on Tuesday 27th March 1979 at 6·30 pm · doors open 6·15·
in the Lecture Theatre · the Victoria & Albert Museum
Cromwell Road · London · SW7
the Chair will be taken by Mr · Ieuan Rees
R·S·V·P Mrs·S·Cavendish · hon Secretary
54 Boileau Road London SW13 9BL

Sydney Day
Invitation to a lecture on *The Book of Kells*. Actual printed size.

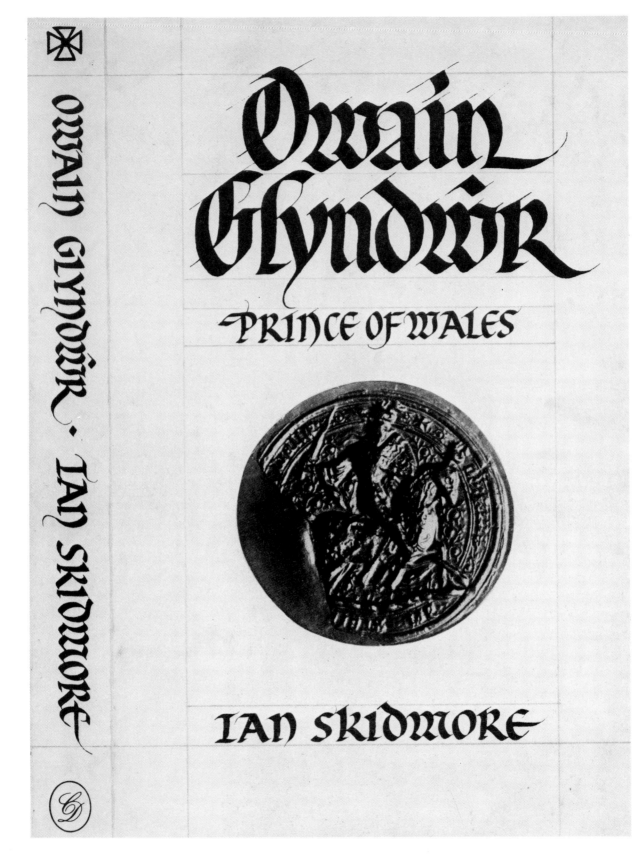

Ieuan Rees
Lettering for a bookjacket. Actual printed
size.

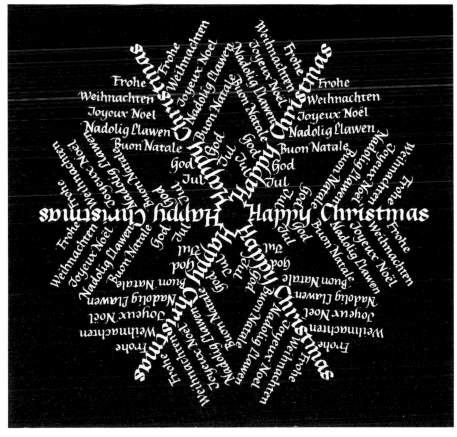

Claude Mediavilla
Calligraphy for a diploma. Original size
30 × 42 cm (12 × 16¾ in).

John Smith
Christmas greetings card. Actual printed
size

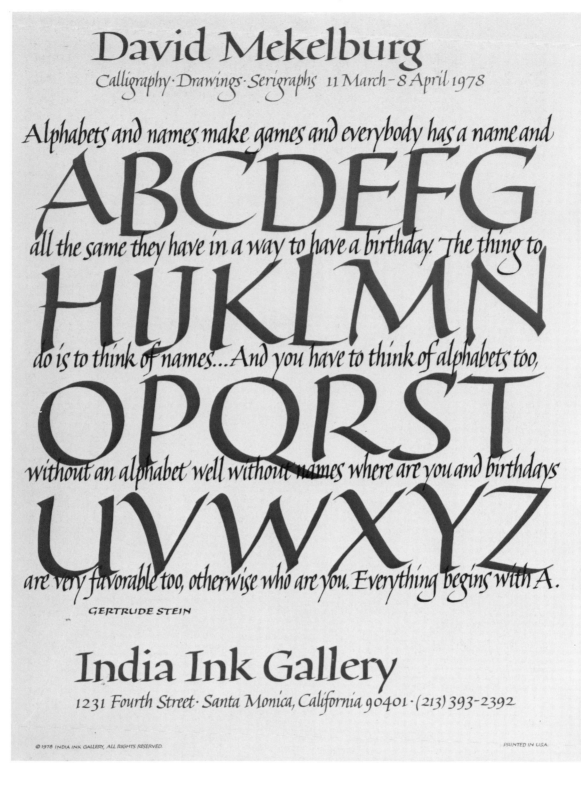

David Mekelburg
Exhibition poster printed in three colours.
Original written out on bond paper with
Automatic and Brause pens. Original and
printed size 60.9 × 45.7 cm (24 × 18 in).

Peter Halliday
'Nursery Maze'. Designed for reproduction as a poster. Printed in black on one colour. Original written out on brown paper in white, yellow and pale green watercolour. Original size 63.5 × 43 cm (25 × 17 in). Printed size 44.4 × 31.7 cm (17½ × 12½ in).

ABCDEF
GHIJKL
MNOP
QRSTU
WXYeZ

Letters are the key to our culture, they can also be a picklock to our heart.

BROR ZACHRISSON

Jacqueline Sakwa
Quotation from Hermann Zapf's *Manmade Typographicum* by Bror Zachrisson, 1954. Written out in dark green gouache on Bodleian hand-made paper. Original size 21.5 × 17.7 cm (8½ × 7 in).

Donald Jackson
Christmas poster. Written out in black stick ink with brush, quill and steel pen on layout paper. Illustrations drawn by Kate Jackson. Height of original 36.7 cm (15 in).

Press advertisement. Written out in stick ink with quill on layout paper. Drawing by Kate and Morgan Jackson. Actual printed size.

Jean Larcher
Logotype for perfume packaging.

Patricia Weisberg
Cover of The Calligraphers' Engagement Calendar 1979, published by Pentalic-Taplinger, New York. Lettering in white reversed out of red. The original was done on bond paper with a Bouwsma pen and touched up for reproduction.

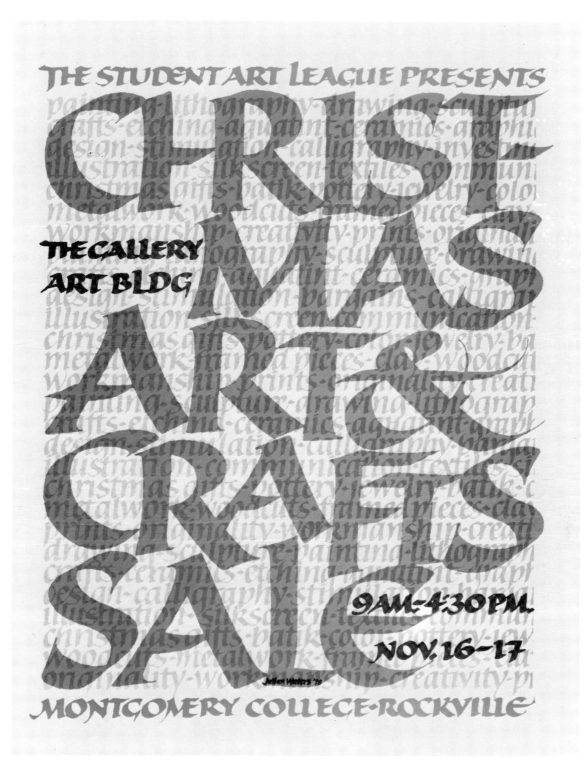

Julian Waters
Poster. Commissioned by Montgomery College, Maryland. Written out in Chinese stick ink with steel nibs and coit pen on hand-made paper. Original size 25 × 19 cm ($9\frac{3}{4}$ × $7\frac{1}{2}$ in).

Julian Waters
Quotation from Shakespeare, *The Tragedy of King Richard III*.I.I. Written out in Chinese stick ink with semi-flexible steel broad edged pens on rough handmade paper. The large capitals were written very small then enlarged photographically to exaggerate roughness. The small capitals were written large and reduced to exaggerate smoothness. Carried out for the 1980 Calligraphers' Engagement Calendar, published by Pentalic Taplinger.

Abigail Diamond Chapman
Calligraphy for the Pentalic-Taplinger Calendar 1979. Original size 21 × 22.8 cm (8¼ × 9 in). Printed size 16.7 × 19 cm (6½ × 7⅞ in).

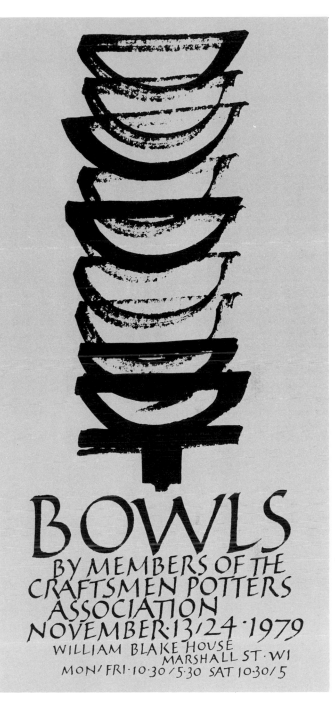

Donald Jackson
Invitation card 'Celia and Hannah'.
Written out in stick ink with quill pen on
layout paper. Original and printed size
21 × 10.4 cm ($8\frac{1}{4}$ × $4\frac{1}{8}$ in).

Invitation card 'Bowls'. Written out in
stick ink, felt tip pen and quills on layout
paper. Original and printed size
22.2 × 10.4 cm ($8\frac{3}{4}$ × $4\frac{1}{8}$ in).

PRIVATE VIEW
Friday 27 October 1978 7·30 pm

Writing and Illuminating & Lettering

AN INTERNATIONAL
EXHIBITION OF
CONTEMPORARY
CALLIGRAPHY

28 October – 18 November 1978
Open weekdays 5pm to 9pm · weekends 2pm to 9pm *

644 Broadway (corner Bleecker)
New York · NY· 10012
(212) 982 5941

* other times by appointment

Charles Pearce
Invitation. Printed size 10.3 × 23.2 cm
(4 × 9⅛ in).

David Graham
Embossed menu cover for luncheon held
in honour of the Royal visit to the Royal
Maundy Service at Winchester Cathedral,
in its 900th anniversary year. Size of menu
24 × 19 cm (9⅞ × 7⅜ in).
Courtesy of the Hampshire County Council.

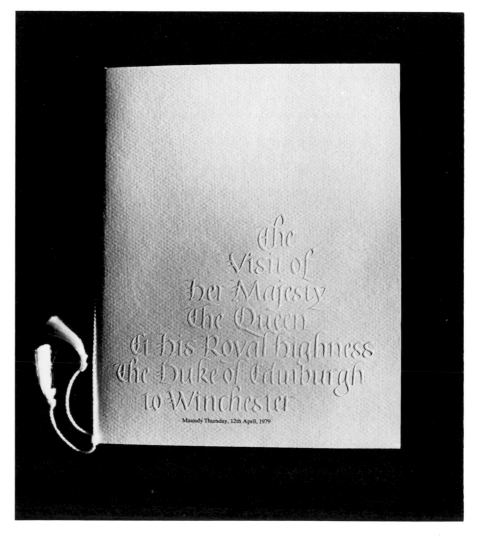

The
Visit of
her Majesty
the Queen
& his Royal highness
the Duke of Edinburgh
to Winchester
Maundy Thursday, 12th April, 1979

David Howells
Lettering for cover of National Trust Calendar.

Donald Jackson
Emblem for use on stationery, flags and Tee-shirts.

Villu Toots
Design for a record sleeve.

Kenneth Breese
Film can label and film titles in brush lettering for Peter Greenaway Films.

Brian P Clare
Logotype designed for the National Commission on the Cost of Medical Care. Original size 15 × 26.2 cm (6 × 10½ in).

David Quay
Logotype designed for Penguin Books.
Original artwork lettered to a width of
20.3 cm (8 in).

Lars Jonsson
Logotype for Swedish rail road
newspaper.

Lars Jonsson
Logotype for a Stockholm gym school.
Award winner in the Type Directors Club
Competition, New York, 1979.

Claude Mediavilla
Logotype designed for an art gallery.

Tony Di Spigna
Design for personal stationery.

Tony Di Spigna
Part of a corporate identity for Johnson's
Sanitation, Minnesota.

I AM A JEW. HATH NOT A JEW EYES ?

HATH NOT A JEW HANDS, ORGANS, DIMENSIONS, SENSES, AFFECTIONS, PASSIONS? FED WITH THE SAME FOOD, HURT WITH THE SAME WEAPONS, SUBJECT TO THE SAME DISEASES, HEALED BY THE SAME MEANS, WARMED AND COOLED BY THE SAME WINTER AND SUMMER AS A CHRISTIAN IS? IF YOU PRICK US, DO WE NOT BLEED? IF YOU TICKLE US, DO WE NOT LAUGH? IF YOU POISON US, DO WE NOT DIE? AND IF YOU WRONG US, SHALL WE NOT REVENGE? IF WE ARE LIKE YOU IN THE REST, WILL RESEMBLE YOU IN THAT.

SHYLOCK · THE MERCHANT OF VENICE · ACT III SCENE I

Abigail Diamond Chapman
Calligraphy for the Pentalic-Taplinger Calendar 1979. Original size 55.8 × 43.1 cm (22 × 17 in). Printed size 16.7 × 14.6 cm (6½ × 5⅞ in).

Jean Larcher
Logotype for an advertising studio in Paris, Five Little Fishes. Art director: Franck Vardon. Original drawn on scratchboard 18 × 61 cm (7 × 23¾ in).

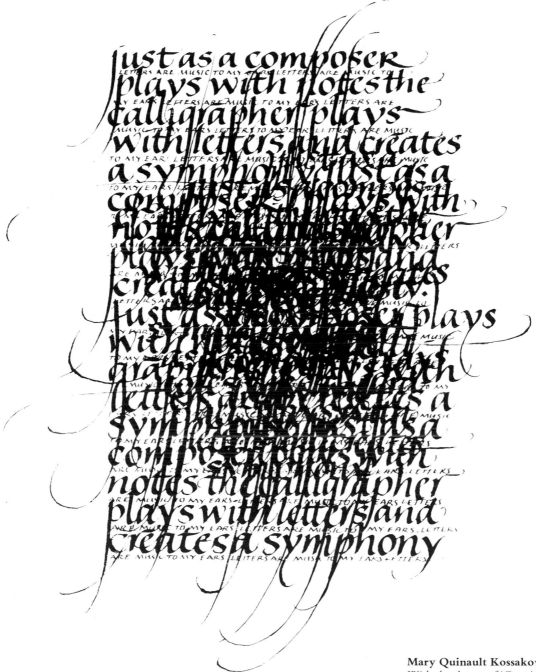

Mary Quinault Kossakowski
With the theme of 'Creativity' this piece
represents an attempt to recreate in letter
forms the feeling of a symphony in
calligraphy thus combining the visual with
audio expression in the arts. Designed for
The Society of Scribes 1979 Calendar.
Written out in Higgins Eternal ink with
two Mitchell broad-edge pens on
Strathmore paper.

The poulterers' shops were still half open and the fruiterers were radiant in their glory. There were great, round, pot-bellied baskets of chestnuts, shaped like the waistcoats of jolly old gentlemen, lolling at the doors, and tumbling out into the street in their apoplectic opulence. There were ruddy, brown-faced, broad-girthed Spanish Onions, shining in the fatness of their growth like Spanish Friars, and winking from their shelves in wanton slyness at the girls as they went by, and glanced demurely at the hung-up mistletoe. There were pears and apples, clustered high in blooming pyramids; there were bunches of grapes, made, in the shopkeepers' benevolence, to dangle from conspicuous hooks, that people's mouths might water gratis as they passed.

Charles Dickens "A Christmas Carol"

Eleanor Winters
Christmas greetings card. Illustration by Linda Dannhauser.

Patricia Weisberg
Calligraphy for the Pentalic-Taplinger Calendar 1979.

Better is a dinner of herbs where love is than a fatted ox and hatred with it.

PROVERBS 15   VERSE 17

PENMAN'S PROGRESS

An exhibition of calligraphy by
Raphael Boguslav

June 17 through July 6, 1978

Reception: Saturday, June 17
3:00 to 5:30 p.m.
You are cordially invited

The Cooper & French Gallery
130 Thames St. Newport R.I.
Phone 401-849-6512,

Raphael Boguslav
Exhibition poster. Printed size
35.5 × 28 cm (14 × 11 in).

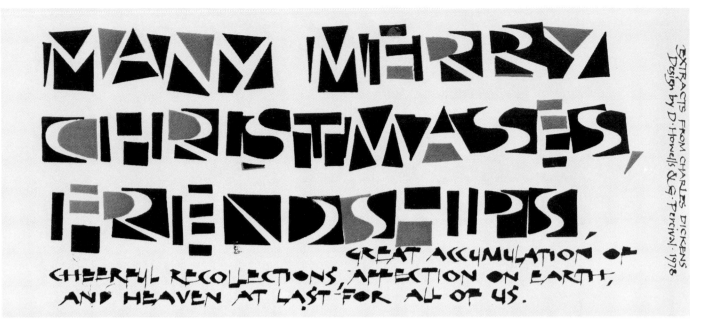

MANY MERRY CHRISTMASSES, FRIENDSHIPS, GREAT ACCUMULATION OF CHEERFUL RECOLLECTIONS, AFFECTION ON EARTH, AND HEAVEN AT LAST FOR ALL OF US.

EXTRACTS FROM CHARLES DICKENS
Design by D. Howells & G. Percival · 1978

In came a fiddler with a music book; and went up to the lofty desk, and made an orchestra of it, and tuned like fifty stomach-aches. In came Mrs. Fezziwig, one vast substantial smile. In came the three Miss Fezziwigs, beaming and lovable. In came the six young followers whose hearts they broke. In came all the young men & women employed in the business. In came the housemaid, with her cousin, the baker. In came the cook with her brother's particular friend, the milkman. In came the boy from over the way, who was suspected of not having board enough from his master; trying to hide himself behind the girl from next door but one, who was proved to have had her ears pulled by her mistress. In they all came, one after another; some shyly, some boldly, some

Such a bustle ensued that you might have thought a goose the rarest of all birds; a feathered phenomenon to which a black swan was a matter of course—and in truth it was something very like it in that house! Mrs. Cratchit made the gravy (ready beforehand in a little saucepan) hissing hot; Master Peter mashed the potatoes with incredible vigour; Miss Belinda sweetened up the apple-sauce; Martha dusted the hot plates; Bob took Tiny Tim beside him in a tiny corner at the table; the two young Cratchits set chairs for everybody, not forgetting themselves, and mounting guard upon their posts, crammed spoons into their mouths.

David Howells and G Percival
Christmas greetings card printed in gold, blue and red. Illustrated here are both sides of card. Printed size 10 × 21.8 cm (4 × 8¼ in).

Inscriptional lettering

NUMBER 1 **MILLBANK**
This plaque was unveiled by
HER MAJESTY THE QUEEN
to commemorate her visit on 6th December, 1978,
marking the thirtieth anniversary of the
amalgamation which formed the
Church Commissioners
for England

David Dewey
Commemorative plaque. Blue grey slate.
45.7 × 45.7 cm (18 × 18 in).

Richard Kindersley
Commemorative plaque commissioned by
The Fishmonger's Company. Carved
Welsh slate. 58 × 46 cm (22½ × 18 in)

David Howells
Modular alphabet. Slip-cast ceramic units
glazed and fixed to a wooden board with
sand-textured surface. 76 cm × 2.1 m
(2 ft 6 in × 7 ft).

Richard Kindersley
Commemorative plaque commissioned by
the Manchester Hospital Board. Carved
Welsh slate. Diameter 66 cm (25¾ in).

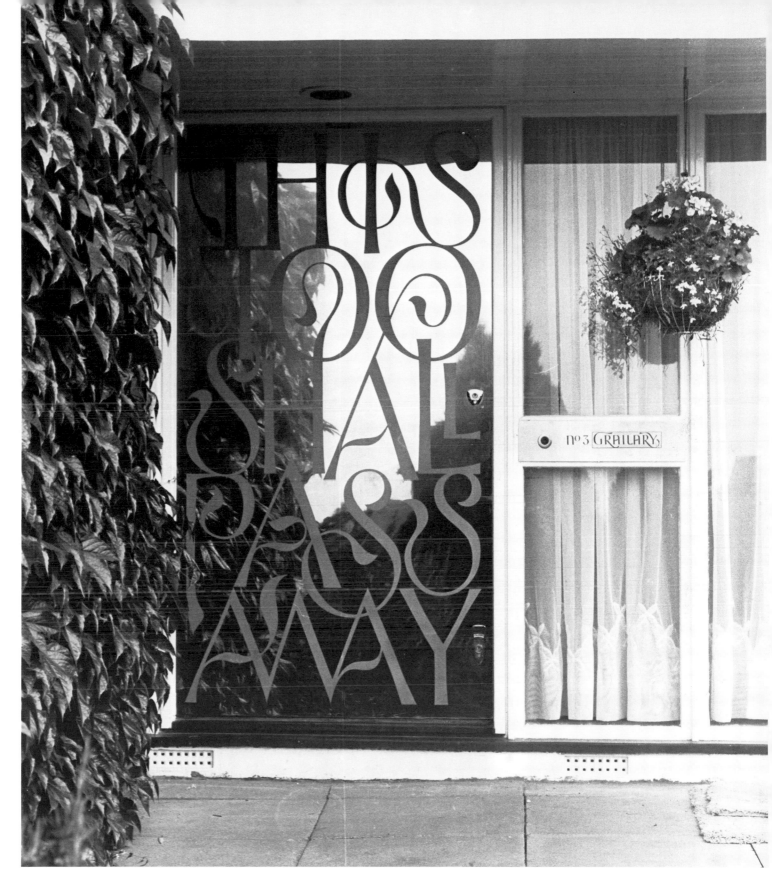

Richard Kindersley
Sand blast stainless steel door.

John Skelton
Sign for the Liquid Paper Corporation,
Dallas, Texas. Riven Buckingham slate.
Brass letters with chrome satin finish.
Length 3.2 m (10 ft 6 in).

TO BE OR NOT TO BE THAT IS THE QUESTION:
WHETHER 'TIS NOBLER IN THE MIND TO SUFFER
THE SLINGS & ARROWS OF OUTRAGEOUS FORTUNE,
OR TO TAKE ARMS AGAINST A SEA OF TROUBLES,
AND BY OPPOSING END THEM? TO DIE: TO SLEEP;
NO MORE; AND BY A SLEEP TO SAY WE END
THE HEART-ACHE & THE THOUSAND NATURAL SHOCKS
THAT FLESH IS HEIR TO. 'TIS A CONSUMMATION
DEVOUTLY TO BE WISH'D. TO DIE: TO SLEEP;
TO SLEEP: PERCHANCE TO DREAM: AY, THERE'S THE RUB;
FOR IN THAT SLEEP OF DEATH WHAT DREAMS MAY COME

Richard Kindersley
Raised lettering in plaster, stained yellow
ochre. 1.3 × 2 m (40 × 78 in).

Sand blast granite, gilded. 30 cm sq
(11¾ in sq).

133

Ieuan Rees
Commemorative plaque for Dyfed
College of Art, Carmarthen. Welsh slate
with sunken oval.

Donald Jackson
Sign of window commissioned by Cranks
Health Foods. Brush painted in
signwriter's enamel. Breadth 61 cm
(24 in). *Courtesy Cranks Health Foods.*

Ieuan Rees
Inscription on two boulders from Penrhyn
Quarry, North Wales. Presented to the
Borough of Brent, London. Height of
tallest boulder approximately 2.4 m (8 ft).

LORD·THOMSON
OF FLEET
1894-1976

*He gave a new direction
to the British newspaper
industry. A strange and
adventurous man from
nowhere, ennobled by the
great virtues of courage
and integrity and
faithfulness*

David Kindersley
Commemorative plaque. Welsh slate, cut
by Kevin Cribb. 99 × 66 cm (39 × 26 in).

Nicolete Gray
Raised letters. Portland stone.

DAFYDD
AP
GWILYM

YR ADFAIL DRAW YW'R
FAN YN ÔL TRADDODIAD
Y GANWYD Y BARDD

YN YSTOD CHWARTER
CYNTAF Y BEDWAREDD
GANRIF AR DDEG

THE RUIN BEYOND IS THE TRADDITIONAL BIRTH-
PLACE OF DAFYDD AP GWILYM (CIRCA 1320-1370),
ONE OF THE GREAT POETS OF MEDIEVAL EUROPE

D'APRÈS LA TRADITION, DAFYDD AP GWILYM
(VERS 1320-VERS 1370), UN DES GRANDS POÈTES
DE L'EUROPE MÉDIÉVALE NAQUIT EN CE LIEU

Ieuan Rees
Inscription in Welsh, English and French.
Welsh blue slate. 88.8 × 127 cm
(1 ft 11 in × 4 ft 2 in).

Lida Lopes Cardozo
Engraved glass roundel. Exhibition piece.

Engraved glass decanter commissioned as
a wedding present for Mr and Mrs David
Jenkins of Oxford. Approximate height
22.8 cm (9 in).

David Kindersley
Rustic Roman letters. Kelton stone, cut
by Lida Lopes Cardozo. 71 × 30.4 cm
(28 × 20 in).

David Kindersley
'Tentoonstelling'. Mansfield limestone, cut
by Kevin Cribb. Approximately
15.2 × 66 cm (6 × 26 in).

Mary White
Wide flanged bowl in porcelain. Dark
green crystally glaze, black centre, gold
lustre lettering. Diameter 32.3 cm (12¾ in).

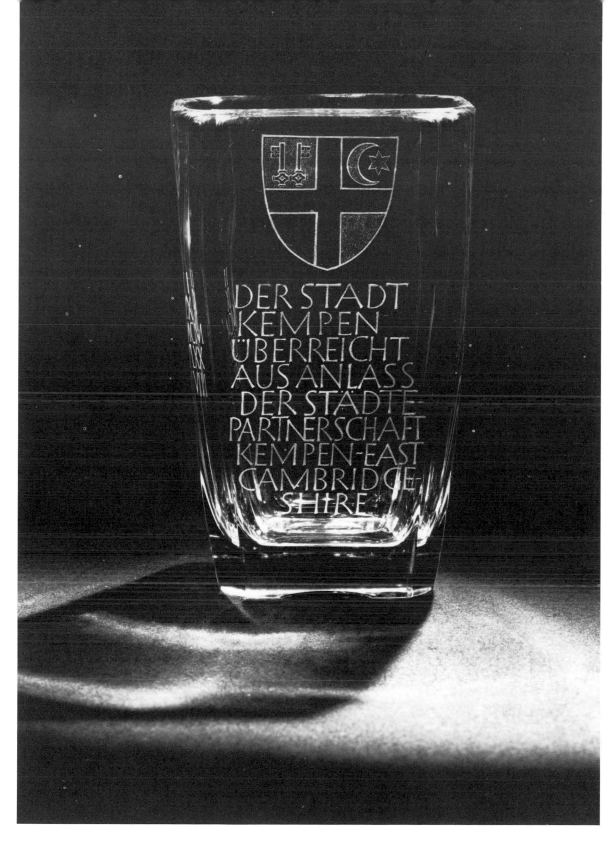

David Peace
Vase engraved in 1978 to mark the twinning of the two local authorities, East Cambridgeshire District Council and Kempen, West Germany. Commissioned by East Cambridge District Council. Height 17.7 cm (7 in).

David Peace
Glass bowl engraved with the lettering
'All embodied labour should be kept in
reverence'. Diameter 30.4 cm (12 in).

David Kindersley
Engraved glass. Cut by Mark Bury.
(26 × 18 in)

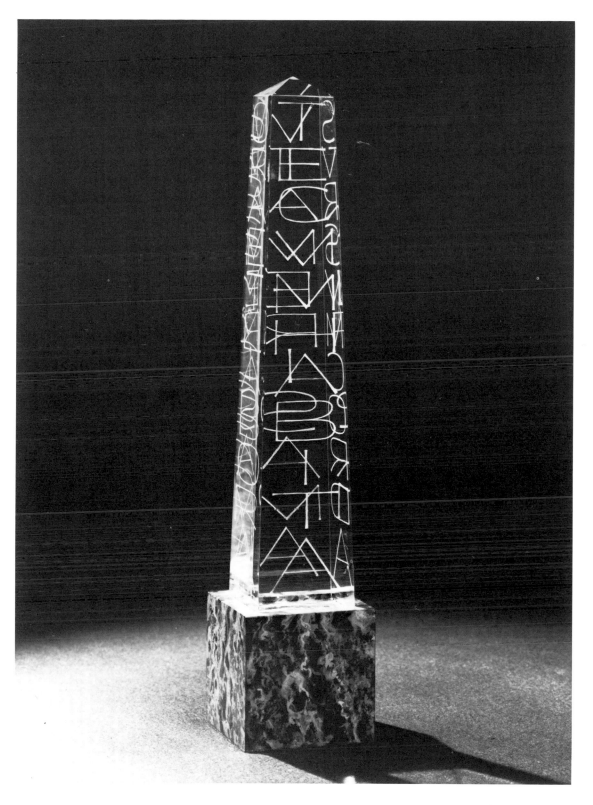

David Peace
Glass obelisk engraved with four Latin
mottoes each of 11 letters ending in 'A':
Ora et Labora; *Sursum Corda*; *Tecum
Habita*; *Ut Ameris Ama*. Overall height
including marble base 30.4 cm (12 in).

Engraved to commemorate the 25th anniversary
of the Accession of Her Majesty Queen Elizabeth II
and the centenary of the Society for the Protection of
Ancient Buildings MCMLXXVII

We
are only
trustees
for
those that
come after
us

WILLIAM MORRIS

&To mark the honour of Patronage of the society
by Her Majesty Queen Elizabeth the Queen Mother
conferred at the celebrations at Euston Hall, 5 July 1977

David Peace
Window pane engraved for the
committee room of the Society for the
protection of Ancient Buildings.

OXFORDSHIRE
COUNTY
MUSEUM
Fletcher's House

The
Bernard Shaw Shop
is named to mark
the bequest to the
British Museum
by George Bernard Shaw
Dramatist, Critic &
Author

David Dewey
Name plaque for Oxford County
Museum. Slate. 61 × 126 cm
(23¾ × 49 in).

John Skelton
Plaque. Welsh slate. Diameter 50.8 cm
(20 in).

John Skelton
Lettering sample. Slate. 22.8 cm sq
(3 ft 6 in).

David Dewey
Slate sign incised and coloured.
69.8 × 61 cm (27½ × 24 in).

John Skelton
Headstone. Red sandstone. Height 1.6 m
(3 ft 6 in).

Harry Meadows
Latin inscription cut in slate.
51 × 30.5 cm (20 × 12 in).

Thomas Perkins
Latin inscription cut in Yorkstone.
Original size 81.2 × 32.3 cm
(32 × 12¾ in).

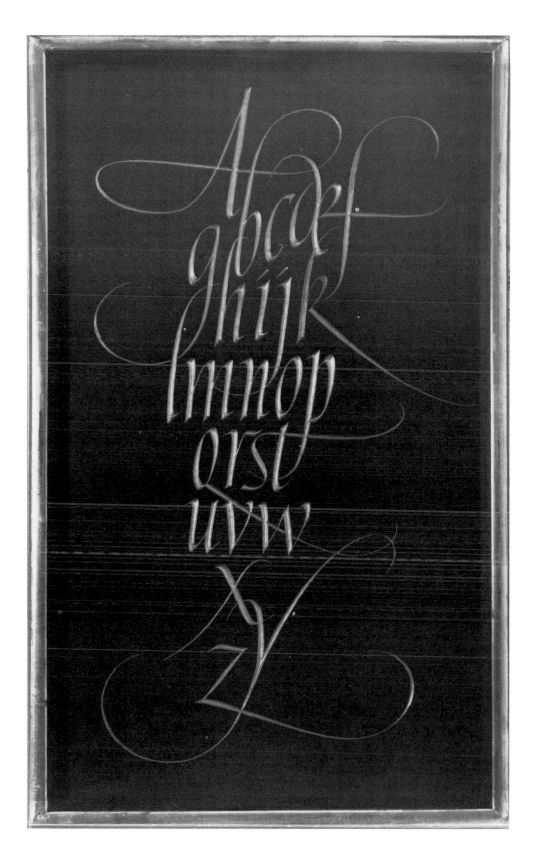

Guillermo Rodriguez–Benitez
Italic alphabet cut in slate.

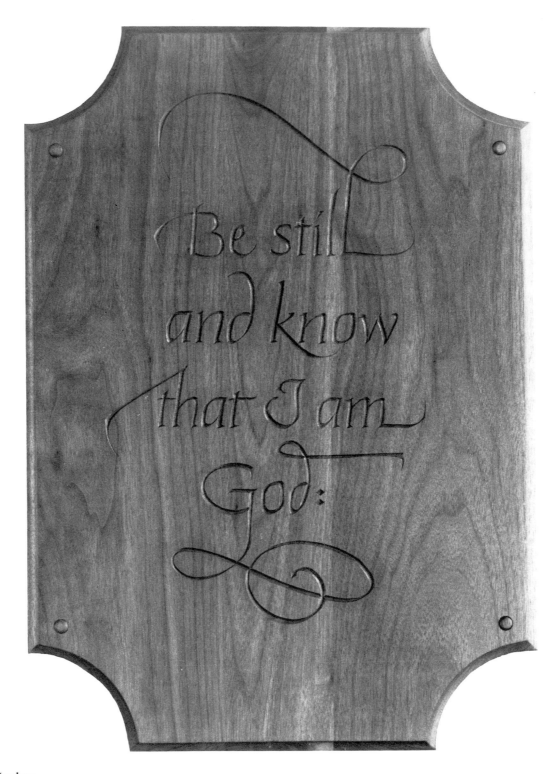

Michael W Hughey
Plaque commissioned by a Church.
American Walnut. 66 × 47.7 cm
(26 × 18 in)

la stampa
nõ possa in tutto
ripresentarte la
Viva mano

John E Benson
Black slate, V-cut gilded letters.
21 × 28.5 cm ($8\frac{1}{2}$ × $11\frac{3}{4}$ in).

John Woodcock
Rings in matching box with engraved lid in silver.

Raymond Gid
'Semaine Sainte'. Medal minted by the
Monnaie de Paris. Both sides shown at
actual size.

152

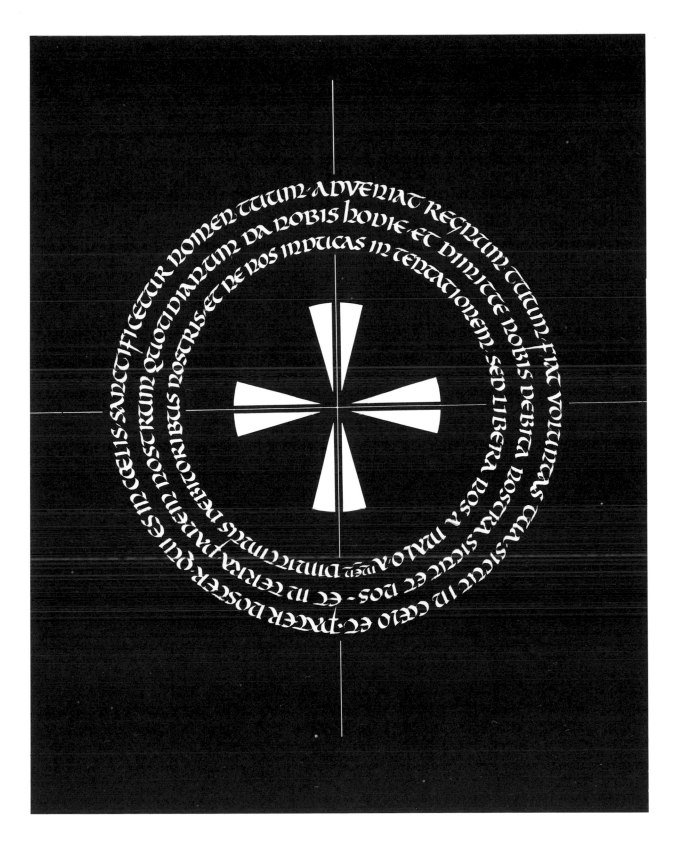

George Thomson
Lord's Prayer. Lettering photo-etched in brass. 25 × 25 cm (9¾ × 9¾ in).

Raymond Gid
'À la Calligraphie Renaissante'. To be
minted as a medal in 1980. Actual size.

'Célébration de la lettre'. Medal minted by
the Monnaie de Paris. Diameter 13.3 cm
(5¼ in).

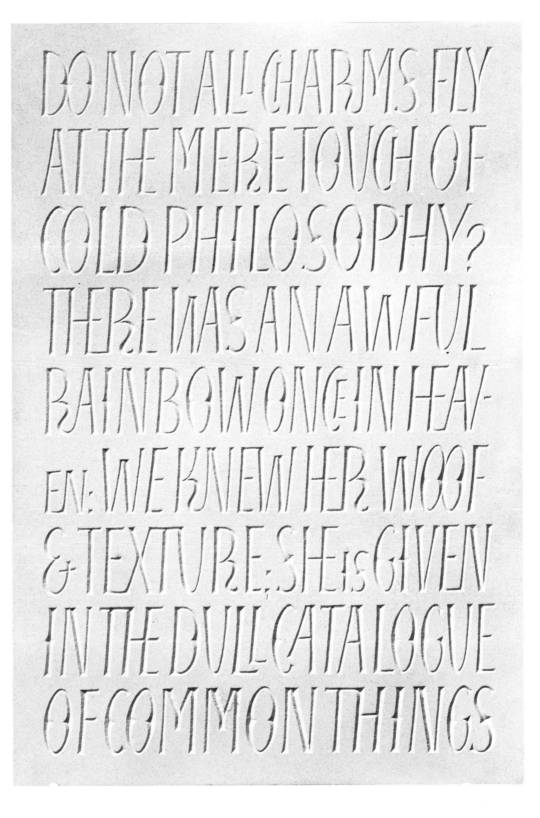

David Kindersley
Plaque engraved with a quotation from
Keats' *Lamia*. Mansfield limestone, cut by
Lida Lopes Cardozo. 73.6 × 48.2 cm
(29 × 19 in).

John E Benson
Black slate, V-cut gilded letters.
70 × 41.2 cm (24 × 16¼ in).

Index of calligraphers

Full addresses of societies or services through which individual
artists can be contacted are given on pages 159–160

Calligraphy societies

Calligraphy societies in USA and Canada

Calligraphers Guild
P.O. Box 304, Ashland, OR 97520

Calligraphy Guild of Pittsburgh
P.O. Box 8167, Pittsburgh, PA 15217

Capital Calligraphers
332 Atwater S, Monmouth, OR 97361

Chicago Calligraphy Collective
P.O. Box 11333, Chicago, ILL 60611

Colleagues of Calligraphy
P.O. Box 4024, St. Paul, MINN 55104

Colorado Calligraphers Guild
Cherry Creek Station, Box 6413, COLO 80206

Escribiente
P.O. Box 26718, Albuquerque, NM 87125

The Fairbank Society
4578 Hughes Road, RR3 Victoria, B.C., Canada V8X 3X1

Friends of Calligraphy
P.O. Box 5194, San Francisco, CA 94101

Friends of the Alphabet
P.O. Box 11764, Atlanta, Georgia 30355

Goose Quill Guild
Oregon State University, Fairbanks Hall, Corvallis, OR 97331

Guild of Bookworkers
663 Fifth Avenue, New York City, NY 10022

Handwriters Guild of Toronto
60 Logandale Road, Willowdale, Ontario, Canada M2N 4H4

Houston Calligraphy Guild
c/o 1024 Willow Oaks, Pasadena, TX 77506

Indiana Calligraphers Association
2501 Pamela Drive, New Albany, IND 47150

Island Scribes
c/o 1000 E 98th Street, Brooklyn, NY 11236

The League of Handbinders
7513 Melrose Avenue, Los Angeles, CA 90046

Lettering Arts Association
303 Cumberland Avenue, Asheville, NC 28801

Lettering Arts Guild of Boston
86 Rockview Street, Jamaica Plain, MA 02130

New Orleans Calligraphers Association
6161 Marquette Place, New Orleans, LA 70118

Opulent Order of Practising Scribes
1310 West Seventh, Roswell, NM 88201

Philadelphia Calligraphers Society
P.B. Box 7174, Elkins Park, PA 19117

Phoenix Society for Calligraphy
1709 North 7th Street, Phoenix, AR 85006

San Antonio Calligraphers Guild
c/o 3118 Mindoro, San Antonio, TX 78217

St. Louis Calligraphy Guild
8541 Douglas Court, Brentwood, MO 63144

St. Petersburg Society of Scribes
c/o 2960 58th Avenue S, St. Petersburg, FLA 33712

Society for Calligraphy & Handwriting
c/o The Factory of Visual Art, 4649 Sunnyside North, Seattle, WA 98103

Society for Calligraphy
P.O. Box 64174, Los Angeles, CA 90064

Society for Italic Handwriting, BC Branch
P.O. Box 48390, Bentall Centre, Vancouver, B.C., Canada V7X 1A2

Calligraphy services

Society of Scribes
P.O. Box 933, New York City, NY
10022

Tidewater Calligraphy Guild
220 Cortland Lane, Virginia Beach, VA
23452

Valley Calligraphy Guild
3241 Kevington, Eugene, OR 97405

Washington Calligraphers Guild
Box 23818, Washington, DC 20024

Western American Branch of the S.I.H.
6800 S.E. 32nd Avenue, Portland, OR
97202

The Western Reserve Calligraphers
3279 Warrensville Center Road, Shaker
Heights, Ohio 44122

Wisconsin Calligraphers' Guild
2124 Kendall Avenue, Madison, WI 53705

Calligraphy societies in Europe

The Society of Scribes & Illuminators
c/o FBCS, 43 Earlham Street, London
WC2H 9LD

The Society for Italic Handwriting
69 Arlington Road, London NW1

The Mercator Society
Gaasterland Str 96, Haarlem, Holland

Bund Deutscher Buchkunstler
6050 Offenbach am Main, Hernstrasse 81,
W. Germany

Calligraphia
5060 Bellaire Avenue, N. Hollywood,
CA 91607

Calligraphics Ink, Inc.
Crystal Underground, Arlington, VA
22202 USA

Calligraphy Design Center
1720 E 86th Street, Indianapolis, IND
46240

Calligraphy Space 2001
644 Broadway, New York City, NY
10012

Scriptorium St. Francis
1323 Cole Street, San Francisco, CA 94117